THE MAGICIAN AND THE SPIRITS

Harry Houdini *and the* Curious Pastime *of* Communicating with the Dead

Deborah Noyes

Viking

VIKING
An imprint of Penguin Random House LLC
375 Hudson Street
New York, New York 10014

First published in the United States of America by Viking,
an imprint of Penguin Random House LLC, 2017

LIBRARY OF CONGRESS CATALOGING-IN-PUBLICATION DATA
Names: Noyes, Deborah, author.
Title: The magician and the spirits : Harry Houdini and the curious pastime
of communicating with the dead / Deborah Noyes.
Description: New York : Viking Books for Young Readers, 2017.
Identifiers: LCCN 2016053762 | ISBN 9780803740181 (hardback)
Subjects: LCSH: Houdini, Harry, 1874–1926—Juvenile literature. |
Magicians—United States—Biography—Juvenile literature. |
Escape artists—United States—Biography—Juvenile literature. | Spiritualism. |
BISAC: JUVENILE NONFICTION / Biography & Autobiography / Historical. |
JUVENILE NONFICTION / Games & Activities / Magic. |
JUVENILE NONFICTION / Social Issues / Death & Dying.
Classification: LCC GV1545.H8 N69 2017 | DDC 793.8092—dc23 LC record
available at https://lccn.loc.gov/2016053762

Printed in China   Set in Revival565 BT   Book design by Kate Renner

10 9 8 7 6 5 4 3 2 1

CONTENTS

INTRODUCTION

Impossibility Commences

Who was Harry Houdini?

Almost everyone has a mental picture of this "mystifier of mystifiers," the most popular magician and escape artist of all time. Whether crouched over handcuffed wrists, liberating himself from a locked jail cell, or making an elephant disappear, he was a blaze of action—a force of mind, muscle, and will. His audiences gaped in wonder as he swallowed needles (or seemed to), bobbed upside down in a water-torture cell, or dangled topsy-turvy in a straitjacket from a tall building.

Over the course of his career, Houdini went by many names. He made his public debut at Jack Hoefler's Five-Cent Circus in 1883, a year after his family settled in Milwaukee, Wisconsin. Billed as Ehrich, the Prince of the Air, the spry acrobat and contortionist was nine years old.

People who saw him later, performing in dime museums,

Harry Houdini, Handcuff King, circa 1905.
Background: A crowd looks up as Houdini performs his
Suspended Straitjacket escape, circa 1916.

sideshows, and jails, and on the big variety stages of vaudeville, knew him variously as King of Cards, Projea the Wild Man, Wizard of Shackles, or the World's Handcuff King and Prison Breaker. As he was quick to advertise, he was an "eclipsing sensation" who left no challenge unanswered. He was known in "every country on the globe," defying "duplication, explanation, imitation or contradiction." And in a life dedicated to dreaming up dazzling tricks, stunts, and escapes, he was his own best invention.

The public knew him by many names but rarely the one he started life with. Born in Budapest, Hungary, in March 1874, Erik Weisz (later Ehrich Weiss) was the son of an impoverished rabbi and a doting mother. Neither parent learned to speak English after immigrating to America, but young Ehrich grew into the picture of New World energy and optimism. He was competitive and ambitious, physically powerful, and powerfully present, all traits that would help shape his career as the consummate showman.

What fewer people know about this most visible of performers is that for decades, Ehrich Weiss (who adopted the stage name Houdini early in his career and would one day autograph his books: "Houdini. That's Enough") was preoccupied with things the eye can't see.

Like many people in the nineteenth and early twentieth centuries, Houdini was intrigued (if not convinced) by the startling idea that spirits not only survive death but can also be contacted and can communicate with the living through a third party called a medium.

THIS BOOK IS THE STORY OF A RATIONAL AND relentless showman whose debunking of deception put him in touch with odd and fascinating characters: mediums who said they could converse with the dead, criminal hucksters, deluded scientists, and committees and investigators with job titles like "Honorary Secretary of the Society for the Study of Supernormal Pictures."

It's also the story of a devoted son devastated by the death of his "Sainted Mother," who swore to investigate spiritual phenomena with an open mind and to uncover and defend truth until the end.

In thirty years, Houdini concluded, in his 1924 book, *A Magician Among the Spirits*, "I have not found one incident that savoured of the genuine."

But it was not for want of trying.

PART ONE

"There Is No Death, There Are No Dead"

ONE

Harry and Bess Houdini, Spirit Mediums

"To me it was a lark." ~*Harry Houdini*

During the late nineteenth and early twentieth centuries, vaudeville—which brought touring novelty acts together on one stage—was the most popular form of entertainment in American cities.

But in remote small towns, where the vaudeville tours wouldn't go, traveling medicine shows and their hodgepodge of players parked their wagons and staged a humbler sort of performance.

The formula was simple: performers took over a street corner, produced musical instruments, and made a racket. Once a crowd gathered, the show's pitchman or "doctor" stepped up on a platform and sold his miraculous potions or elixirs. Often he invited the audience back to a local auditorium or music hall for more marvels and "medicine" the same evening.

In late 1897, in need of steady work, twenty-three-year-old Harry Houdini and his young bride, Bess—both struggling variety performers—signed on for a fifteen-week tour with "Dr."

Thomas Hill's California Concert Company, a typical traveling Midwestern medicine show, at twenty-five dollars a week.

The company, which included Swiss bell ringers, a German comedian, and the many-talented Keatons (family of future silent-film star Buster Keaton), gathered on dusty street corners in Kansas and Oklahoma Territory to draw crowds. Houdini (billed as the "Great Wizard") thumped a tambourine, Bess (the "little vocalist") sang, and when enough curious onlookers had gathered, Dr. Hill announced the evening's show and went to work peddling bottled potions.

The season started out well, but at some point audiences began to dwindle. Dr. Hill had heard of other Midwestern shows drawing crowds with séance and mind-reading routines. Would Houdini want to develop a psychic act of his own?

The Great Wizard had seen a few spirit demonstrations in New York and had no high opinion of them. But for a magician with a mind for mechanics, they would be easy to duplicate, and if

Bess and Harry Houdini in their first year of marriage, 1894.

Houdini could help the show prosper, it was worth a try.

Before a performance one evening in Garnett, Kansas, he visited the local cemetery, "accompanied by the sexton and the oldest inhabitant of the town." He

A medicine-show pitchman attracts a crowd in Huntingdon, Tennessee, 1935.

surveyed the graves, jotting down names and ages from the stones. "I had a notebook," Houdini later recalled in a lecture exposing such deceptions, and if the words carved in marble or granite said too little, "the sexton would tell me the missing data, and the old Uncle Rufus would give me the scandals of everyone sleeping in God's acre."

Houdini spent the day mingling with townsfolk and asked discreet questions. People were only too happy, he learned, to gossip

☞ The Houdinis

After a brisk courtship of three weeks, Harry Houdini married Wilhelmina Beatrice "Bess" Rahner, a slight pixie of a girl who sang in an act called the Floral Sisters.

Though Harry's mother accepted the bride at once, Bess's mother, a Catholic, couldn't forgive her daughter for marrying into a Jewish family, and shunned Bess for nearly a decade.

The honeymoon on Coney Island was "cheap" but "glorious," said Bess. Billed as the Houdinis, the newlyweds now became partners onstage as well as off.

Harry and Bess were devoted for life, despite a few bumps in the road, and he showered her with gifts and little love notes, addressed to "Darling One and Only" and "Precious Lump of Sweetness."

"Every morning," Bess recalled, "I would find a dear funny little Message like [this] on my pillow."

about themselves and their neighbors.

The afternoon crowd had already seen Houdini escape leg irons and handcuffs, and Dr. Hill had hinted, too, at the young man's extraordinary gift for communicating with the dead. Intrigued, much of the same crowd—and quite a few newcomers—flocked to the local opera house that night to see and hear Houdini in action. He gave them what they came for. Hurling off the ropes that bound him in his chair, he strode downstage as applause faded and the audience grew hushed and uneasy.

In a low, thrilling voice, Houdini mused about the spirit world. Like other performers of the day who included psychic themes (telepathy, hypnosis, mediumship) in their acts, he primed the audience. He closed and opened his eyes. He trembled and gasped as if sensing an invisible presence Words were coming through, he said—names and dates. As his gaze roamed the room, his voice caught to build drama. One by one, he delivered "messages" from Beyond, revealing facts and family secrets that only a handful of people in the community could have known.

Houdini and Bess also did a joint mind-reading act. Bess walked

☞ The Effect

Magicians often buy or inherit the secrets and apparatus, or equipment, of retiring performers, and Houdini got his Metamorphosis trick this way for twenty-five dollars (a heap of cash at the time). The illusion included a "substitution" trunk—a steamer trunk big enough to hold a person, with airholes—a giant curtained cabinet, and instructions.

Houdini would begin by calling an audience committee onstage. While they examined the props, he stepped into a black flannel sack inside the open steamer trunk. His volunteers taped the mouth of the bag shut. They closed and padlocked the trunk, swaddled it in thick, knotted rope, sealed the knots with wax, and then wheeled it into the curtained cabinet while Houdini thumped and hollered inside to prove he was still there.

"Now then," called Bess, stepping into the cabinet with

the trunk. "I shall clap my hands three times . . . I ask you to watch closely for the—EFFECT." At the third clap, she whisked the curtain closed. Assistant and trunk disappeared behind the fabric. But almost instantly, the curtain opened again, and out stepped Houdini. Volunteers raced to undo the rope and unlock the trunk. The flannel bag was still inside, still tied up with tape— and inside that? Bess. The baffled audience cheered wildly as a member of the committed extended a hand to help Houdini's nimble assistant to her feet.

"Just think over this," Houdini boasted in one of their ads. "The time consumed in making the change is THREE SECONDS!"

It was a feat perfectly suited to Bess's quick, slight frame and Houdini's muscular dexterity. The Houdinis' signature act was a spectacle with staying power.

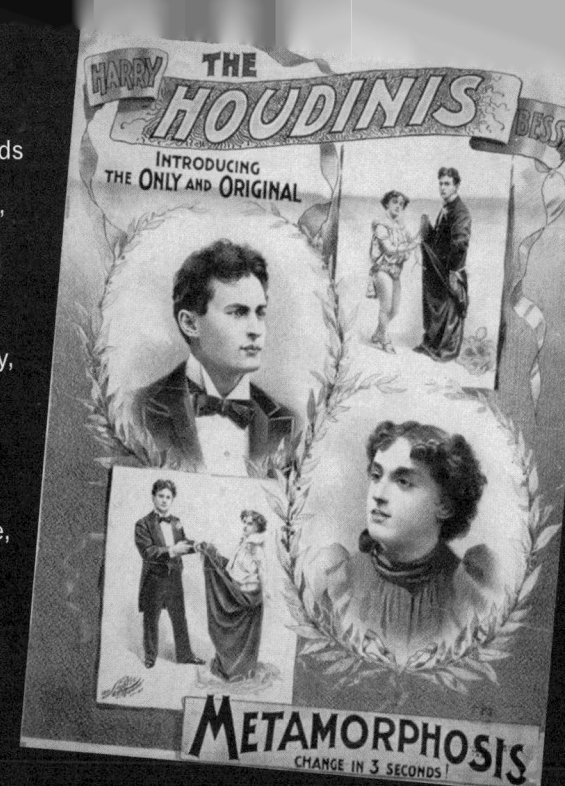

A theatrical poster advertising the Houdinis' Metamorphosis act, circa 1895.

The couple performed it together on and off for years, even after Houdini's solo career took off.

into the crowd and took a dollar bill from an audience member, challenging Houdini to divine its serial number. Her husband concentrated with otherworldly intensity and then, as the crowd hummed with excitement, rattled it off, digit by slow digit. It was all a clever trick—the Houdinis had devised silent and spoken codes for such occasions—but audiences were convinced.

*Undated advertisement for the Houdinis'
early Spiritualist act.*

Dr. Hill's own spirits were high when he tallied the receipts, and soon, the California Concert Company was staging spirit acts in a different town each Sunday.

But the Houdinis' success as fake mediums and mind readers alone couldn't save Hill's operation. In early 1898, the medicine show collapsed, and the young couple set out on their own, booking small venues where Harry performed escapes and the duo continued to fine-tune their best-known magic act, Metamorphosis, the "greatest and finest Trunk Mystery the world has ever seen."

They didn't banish the "spirits" from the show, though. They also incorporated spectral messages, mind reading, and levitating tables, sometimes billing themselves as "The Great Mystifier" and "The Celebrated Psycrometic Clairvoyant."

"I appreciated the fact that I surprised my clients," Houdini later wrote, "but

Welsh Bros Circus season 1896
. Great 10 cent circus in out of way places he played to 25¢ audiences

Harry and Bess Houdini with the Welsh Brothers Circus, 1896.

while aware of the fact that I was *deceiving* them I did not see or understand the seriousness." For the time being, he approached the work in a spirit of play. He was living "like a king," after all, compared to life before séances and mind reading, earning much-needed income by posing as a channel between the living and the dead.

The Houdinis spent several more years performing a mish-mash of routines in small circuses, music halls, and dime museums (a popular form of "lowbrow" entertainment that brought scientific curiosities and shameless thrills under the same roof). Often changing or renaming their routine as they struggled to find the formula for making it in show business,

Harry and Bess had yet to focus and refine the act that would eventually put his talents in the forefront, with Bess stepping back into a supporting role.

By 1899, Houdini was ready to pack it in, give up magic altogether, and resort to teaching others the tricks of his trade. He and Bess moved back to New York to live with his mother, but

A sideshow poster circa 1885 advertising Count Orloff, the stage name of Ivannow Wladislaus von Dziarski-Orloff (1864– 1904), who suffered from an unknown wasting disease that made his skin transparent.

☞ Miraculous Mentors

During Houdini's hungry years on the dime-museum circuit, he formed lasting friendships with many of the "freaks"—stars like Count Orloff, the Transparent Man or Human Window Pane ("You Can See His Heart Beat! You Can See His Blood Circulate!")—who attracted big crowds and bigger salaries. In his 1920 book, *Miracle Mongers and Their Methods*, Houdini pays tribute to fire-eaters, glass chewers, sword-, stone-, and umbrella-swallowers, and "defiers of poisonous reptiles," performers like the Incombustible Spaniard, the Human Ostrich, and the Electric Girl. "The dime museum is but a memory now," he wrote. In three generations he believed it would be completely forgotten. Bess often refused to play the dime museums; vaudeville offered more money, stability, and respectability for the young couple. But Houdini learned some handy tricks there.

Harry still had advance bookings to honor, and while performing at a beer hall in St. Paul, Minnesota, he got the break performers dream of. A big-shot manager, vaudeville tycoon Martin Beck, saw his routine and challenged Houdini to escape from a series of handcuffs.

Houdini proved himself with gusto, and on March 14, Beck sent a telegram from Chicago: "You can open Omaha March twenty sixth sixty dollars, will see act probably make you proposition for all next season."

Houdini kept the telegram and later scribbled on it for posterity: "This wire changed my whole Life's journey."

In a year's time, he would be on his way to becoming a household name, a famed star of American entertainment . . . but certainly not as a mind-reading spirit conjurer.

TWO

Dealings with the Dead

"Spiritualism is the Science, Philosophy and Religion of continuous life, based upon the demonstrated fact of communication, by means of mediumship, with those who live in the spirit world." ∼ SPIRITUALIST MANUAL
OF THE NATIONAL SPIRITUALIST
ASSOCIATION OF CHURCHES

People have believed since ancient times that spirits can survive death and exist outside the body. This wasn't a new idea—even back in 1848—but the popular religious movement known as Spiritualism got its start in that year with two bored young girls.

No one could explain the strange rapping and bumping noises that were coming from the walls and floor of the Fox farmhouse in Hydesville, New York. John and Margaret Fox hadn't slept for days and were already jumpy on the evening their children—Maggie, fourteen, and Kate, eleven—made a show of rapping back.

When the sounds started up as usual that chill March night, their youngest sat up in bed and repeatedly snapped her fingers. The intruding presence—in later reports, Kate called him "Mr. Splitfoot"—rapped back the same number.

The Fox sisters (left to right: Maggie, Kate, and Leah).

Not to be outdone, Maggie cried, "Now do this just as I do," and clapped her hands four times. Four brisk raps followed.

A frightened Mrs. Fox called in neighbors to bear witness. The crowd devised a simple code by pairing a set number of raps to each letter of the alphabet; using it, the ghostly communicator claimed to belong to the corpse of a murdered peddler buried beneath the house.

Men took to the cellar with picks and shovels and dug for days but hit groundwater and had to stop. A flood of pilgrims arrived, meanwhile, on foot, in rented carriages, and by horse and buggy. They pitched tents and trampled the fields around the farmhouse, lit bonfires, peered in the family's windows, and trickled in at night for their turn with the spirit while Maggie, Kate, and Mrs. Fox interpreted.

When public curiosity assumed the proportions of an invasion, John and Margaret shipped the children off to relations. Not surprisingly, wherever the sisters went, the raps went, too. The girls proved able to enter a trance state and confer with those on the "other side."

Before long, sensing an opportunity, their much-older sister, Leah, got involved. A struggling single mother who taught piano in Rochester, Leah had access to the city's progressive elite. Her pupils were the children of Quakers, suffragists, abolitionists, and other social reformers, forward thinkers open to spirit communication and the bold possibilities it suggested. At a time when the United States was mending from civil war and growing fast, Spiritualism—which straddled the boundary between science and magic—seemed to many a visionary movement destined to help rebuild society during a period of political and religious uncertainty.

Within a year, the Fox sisters were showing off their strange talents at Corinthian Hall, Rochester's public auditorium, with hundreds lining up at dawn to hear the "rappings" and witness spirit phenomena.

Ambitious—and by Maggie's report, exploitative—Leah became her younger sisters' official manager, guiding their shared career as celebrity mediums, booking demonstrations in Manhattan and around the country, and spreading the gospel of Spiritualism.

☞ Where Do We Go from Here?

Spiritualism exploded around the time of the Civil War in America, when death was a profoundly visible fact of life. At the same time, scientific progress was indirectly challenging religious doctrine. In his revolutionary 1859 book, *On the Origin of Species*, geologist and naturalist Charles Darwin theorized that life on earth was created not all at once but over billions of years. Plants and animals descended and adapted from common ancestors in the way-distant past, he proposed, which many read as an attack on God's creation of all living beings as described in the Bible. If the very origins of the earth and humankind were in question, what other religious beliefs were at risk? What about eternal life and heaven? His theory of evolution by natural selection was a revelation so startling, Darwin admitted, that writing it was "like confessing a murder." The Fox sisters had tapped into growing public unease and a longing for evidence that death wasn't the end and that the dead were not lost.

Charles Darwin, circa 1858.

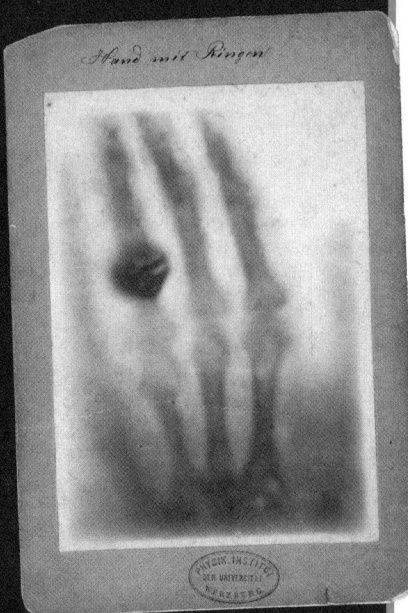

The first medical X-ray, 1895.

✍ Light and Marvels

Throughout the century and into the new millennium, scientific advances and unseen forces—the telegraph, the radio, X-rays, electricity, and radioactivity—seemed like miracles to the average person. If invisible light could show the skeleton beneath flesh, if messages could travel on electrical wires across an ocean, who could rule out the possibility that human intelligence lived on and could be contacted after death or that the departed might be eager to talk back? Along with pastimes like mesmerism (hypnotism) and phrenology (the study of human personality using the shape and character of the skull), Spiritualism had found its moment.

The fever spread. With its promise of a direct channel to the divine and to lost ones "beyond the veil," Spiritualism was especially attractive to mothers in an era when women primarily oversaw the home. In New York State, some half of deaths were of children under five. Grieving parents sought consolation in the Spiritualist idea that death wasn't an end but a change, like a caterpillar becoming a butterfly. Believers wore white at funerals, where mediums fielded messages from souls relocated to Summerland, the Spiritualist name for heaven.

Soon it seemed everyone was hosting parlor séances, delivering messages from Beyond, tipping tables, levitating objects, and conjuring spirits. By 1853, there were tens of thousands of spirit mediums at work, and Maggie and Kate Fox, the movement's figureheads, were the most famous of all.

Like magicians and other performers, the sisters toured a more or less established circuit, conducting séances in hotel

Theatrical poster advertising magician Harry Kellar, 1894.

suites and performing demonstrations in auditoriums around the country and abroad. Along the way, they encountered acclaim but also suspicion and intolerance, even threats of violence.

The worst of their detractors branded them witches or plotted to tar and feather them. More civilized skeptics elected investigators and committees. These challenged the girls to produce their raps under scientific test conditions, a process that could involve humiliating searches or having their wrists and ankles bound. But the Fox sisters kept investigators and audiences guessing, and their fame grew. (It would be decades before Maggie revealed their methods, in a stunning 1888 confession at New York's Academy of Music, and they were fully "exposed.")

Onstage or in a packed music hall, Spiritualist phenomena made for good theater. It took place in the dark, and "manifestations" were eerie and thrilling. Magicians soon jumped on the bandwagon, borrowing Spiritualist tricks and "apparatus"—equipment and props like luminous hands, floating spirit lights, and unfurling curtains—to up the drama at their own shows.

Golden-age magicians (mid-1800s–1920s) like Harry Kellar, Robert Heller, and Howard Thurston appeared to conjure spirits, get teakettles talking in ghostly whispers, or summon bloody script on their bare arms. It was a mutually beneficial arrangement: showmen borrowed from Spiritualists; Spiritualists borrowed from showmen.

Ghostly effects became so common at magic shows that in his 1868 book, *Les Secrets de la prestidigitation et de la magie* (*The Secrets of Conjuring and Magic*), pioneering French magician Jean Eugène Robert-Houdin designated "the Medium Business—Spiritualism" as one of the six branches of conjuring.

Inspired by the investigations mediums like the Fox sisters endured to prove their abilities, magicians working with spirit themes brought audience-controlled test conditions into shows voluntarily. They had themselves bound with rope, closed into trunks or cabinets, or handcuffed to suggest to audiences that their feats

☞ An Earnest, Lifelong Endeavor

When young Ehrich Weiss set out to be a professional magician in the early 1890s, he took the stage name Harry Houdini. "Harry" echoed his childhood nickname, "Ehrie." "Houdini" was a nod to his idol, French magician Jean Eugène Robert-Houdin (1805–1871).

Known as the father of modern magic, Robert-Houdin made the stereotype of the fusty old "wizard" in trailing robes vanish. He cut an elegant figure onstage in formal eveningwear, and his effects were inventive, dazzling audiences with electricity, mag-

netism, and automata (clockwork figures).

In his 1858 memoirs, *Confidences d'un prestidigitateur* (published in English as *Memoirs of Robert-Houdin*), Robert-Houdin describes his worldly adventures, his rise as a sophisticated performer, and his thoughts on magic as an evolving art form. Houdini pored over these pages, and Robert-Houdin became his "guide and hero," lending magic "a dignity worth attaining at the cost of earnest, life-long endeavor."

But his adoration wouldn't last.

were magic—not mere sleight of hand—and that they weren't up to mischief in the dark.

But, of course, they *were*. Stage mediums and magicians who produced their phenomena under test conditions were early "escape artists." Under cover of darkness, or otherwise concealed, they freed themselves long enough to creep from their seats, create effects, and steal back again, giving the impression that they hadn't budged, and the credit went to spirits.

Ira and William Davenport, billed as the Davenport brothers, performed one of the most famous spirit acts. With their quiet stage presence, twin goatees, great drooping mustaches, and signature mahogany cabinet, they bewildered audiences by having a committee from the crowd shut them up in the cabinet, lashed to their chairs with a shelf of musical instruments inside. Raised

Within a decade, Houdini would reduce the man he'd crowned "The Shakespeare of Magic" to the "prince of pilferers."

When he set out to write "The First Authentic History of Magic Ever Published," an encyclopedia of great magicians, Houdini regretted to inform readers that the legendary Robert-Houdin was "a mere pretender" who "waxed great on the brainwork of others." Published in 1908 with the title *The Unmasking of Robert-Houdin*, Houdini's encyclopedia turned into a ruthless exposé of his former hero. All the master's signature effects, he claimed, hailed from earlier magicians.

Colleagues winced at this assault. Some published counterarguments. Magicians in France read Houdini's attack as a national insult. The brash American did more than question his elder's honor and originality; he denied that Robert-Houdin had brought about "a complete regeneration in the art of conjuring" and accused him of exaggeration and "supreme egotism," charges often leveled at Houdini himself.

Robert-Houdin had dropped in his esteem, but it was too late to drop the name. In fact, in 1913, Ehrich Weiss legally changed his name to Harry Houdini, one of the most famous titles in the world.

and set back from the wall to rule out trapdoors (through which stealthy "confederates" might steal in to assist), the cabinet was seven feet long and six feet high, with three doors. The volunteers formed a tense circle around it all through the presentation to bar against trickery, but once the doors closed, a racket sounded: guitar strings vibrated, tambourines tinkled and thumped, and bells jangled. When the doors opened again, there sat the dead-pan brothers, their bonds intact, the musical instruments quiet again on their shelves.

The secret to their success (the "Davenport Rope Tie") was closely guarded, and Spiritualists and skeptics squabbled over the nature of the brothers' gifts. Were they true psychics? Or just ingenious players? The brothers kept the truth under their hats, letting audiences form their own conclusions. This added mystery to mystification, and wherever they went, applause and

The Davenport brothers and William Fay with their spirit cabinet, circa 1908.

The cabinet trick offered by the Davenport Brothers. From an old print in the Harry Houdini Collection.

headlines awaited. So did controversy, angry mobs, brawls, and lawsuits.

At a tour stop in Liverpool, England, the brothers complained that the ropes the audience had used to bind their hands were too tight, stopping their circulation, and had an assistant cut them loose. Feeling cheated by brash American showmen, the crowd smashed the brothers' cabinet to pieces, and a riot broke out. Splinters from the famous wardrobe were later sold in the street as souvenirs.

The Davenports regularly performed for royalty—from Napoleon III and Czar Alexander II to Queen Victoria. They were sensational and dramatic and admired by fellow magicians, including Houdini, who would one day befriend

MISS UNDINA

in ihren neuen sensationellen · Entfisselungs-Act aus der Fussfolter (unter Wasser!)

Theatrical poster advertising Miss Undina with her version of Houdini's Water-Torture Cell Escape.

☞ Fifty-Five Kings

Houdini insisted on setting himself apart from other magicians, but his rivals—to his profound irritation—copied him anyway, trading on his hard work. Despite his threats and protests, imitators with names like "Hourdene," "Whodini," "Cutini," and "Stillini" swiped his handcuff and water-torture methods, his wardrobe style and press poses, and even his publicity. On tour in England, he heard of some fifty-five Kings of Handcuffs: "If you throw a stone in the air," he grumped, "it will fall down and hit someone who has a handcuff key in his pocket." Houdini pasted competitors' ads and reviews in his scrapbooks and would spy on, humiliate, and ruin them if he could, even spill their secrets (the cardinal sin of magicians). "If you are in a fight," he once said, "hit the other guy first."

the elderly Ira and, during a 1910 visit to Australia (where Ira's brother had died in 1877), spruce up William Davenport's neglected gravesite.

By the time young Harry and Bess Houdini turned up on a street corner in Garnett, Kansas—fifty years after the eerie raps on the walls of a farmhouse in Hydesville—the play between mediums and magicians was a long-established tradition.

Houdini was nothing if not an original ("With due mod-

Houdini in chains, circa 1900.

⚐ Naked Ambition

Houdini's escapes were strenuous and clever, he'd admit, but they were about bodybuilding and burglary skills, not psychic talent. Houdini almost always worked in broad daylight, giving the impression that his feats were an open book—more method than magic. He often left his bonds or casings undisturbed; the crate he'd escaped from remained mysteriously nailed shut, the jail cell still locked. And like high-profile mediums—who were often taken aside and searched in the nude before a séance to ensure they weren't smuggling in props—Houdini tackled jail escapes in the buff. No one could accuse him, then, of sneaking keys or lock-picking tools into a cell.

esty," as he put it, "I recognize no one as my peer") and, with Martin Beck guiding his vaudeville career, distanced himself from the medium business early on. He borrowed its escape element, but made it his own, repeatedly outdoing himself while never claiming (or silently letting his audience suppose, as the Davenports did) that his feats were paranormal.

The success of his early spirit act with Bess is no surprise, but neither is the fact that Houdini cut the talking dead from his show.

Deceiving the public as a fake spirit medium never sat well with him. His father and an older brother had died when Houdini was a young man, and it may be that he felt real empathy for his "marks," often people mourning the loss of a loved one. "I most certainly did not relish the idea," he said, "of treading on the sacred feelings of my admirers."

And in 1913, he suffered another loss, one that would lay the groundwork for, if not exactly trigger, the crusade of a lifetime a decade later.

THREE

The Mother's Boy

"I who have laughed at the terrors of death, who have smilingly leaped from high bridges, received a shock from which I do not think recovery is possible." ~*Harry Houdini*

Houdini woke early on the summer morning in 1913 when he and Bess would sail from Hoboken, New Jersey, to Hamburg, Germany, for a European tour. From Hamburg, the partners would continue on to Copenhagen, Denmark, by rail. Houdini would perform for the king of Sweden at the palace in Stockholm and also make a stop in Budapest, where he was born.

But first, there were good-byes.

Finding it difficult to leave his adored mother, Cecilia Weiss, behind on the dock as he and Bess boarded, Houdini kept circling back, dimly aware that Cecilia's health was failing, that "the Great Dissolution was gradually taking place." As paper streamers rained down all around, and the crowd began to sort itself into passengers on deck and well-wishers below, he was magnetically drawn to the spot where his mother stood in her dark

Houdini with Bess and his mother, Cecilia Steiner Weiss, 1907.

clothes beside his mother-in-law and one of his older brothers, Bill—specks in a vast, milling crowd.

"Ma was worried and told me to remain on board," he wrote later, "but I kept coming back and embracing her." When he kissed her good-bye, his mother met his eyes and said, in German, "Ehrich, perhaps I won't be here when you return." She had said such things before, so he joked it off, and she steered the conversation to ordinary matters, asking him to fetch her back a pair of woolen slippers from overseas, size six.

"All right, Mama," agreed Houdini, a devoted son, but he couldn't shake his unease. As the German steamer *Kronprinzessin Cecilie* (*Crown Princess Cecilia*) chuffed out of the harbor, Cecilia Weiss grew smaller, obscured by the crowd.

ABOUT A WEEK LATER, HOUDINI AND BESS TOOK A midnight train to Copenhagen for his first performance. His assistant, Franz Kukol, had given him a cable sent from Asbury Park, New Jersey, where some of the Weiss family were vacationing, but he didn't read it until he reached Circus Beketow, where he would play for an audience including the princes of the royal family. He opened the cable during a press conference, and the news was devastating: his mother had died the night before, following a stroke. Houdini, who was already suffering from an ailing kidney, collapsed on the spot.

When he came to, he wept inconsolably. A doctor had been called in to consult about his kidney, and Houdini ignored orders to admit himself at the hospital for tests.

He canceled all engagements, booked passage for the *Crown Princess Cecilia*'s return voyage, and cabled his younger brother Theo to postpone the funeral.

Before he and Bess set out for Hamburg and departure, Houdini found another unopened cable from Theo, an earlier message urging him to catch a steamer back. Their mother was stricken, it said; there was no hope; he should return home at once if he wanted to say good-bye.

It was already too late, and the strained farewell dockside in Hoboken would be Houdini's last memory of the person arguably dearest to him in the world.

At his request, and against Jewish tradition and law, which require burial within a day after death, Cecilia Weiss's corpse was not buried immediately. Although tradition forbids display of the body, she was laid out for viewing when Houdini arrived.

Her form looked to him dainty and small, her features "still and quiet." It was strange, Houdini wrote later, to see his industrious mother "resting for the first time in 'Her Earthly Career.'" Houdini brought a chair from her room and sat by her body all night.

Before she was buried the next day beside his father, Mayer Samuel Weiss, at Cypress Hills (Machpelah) Cemetery in Queens, New York, Houdini tucked the wool slippers he had brought her from Denmark into his mother's coffin.

The weeks that followed found him "bowed down." It was all he could do to rouse himself and return to Europe to make good on old bookings.

In Germany, Houdini collected into a single volume the letters written by his "Sainted Mother." Each read to him like "a prayer" for her children, "a plea that we should be good human beings." The letters often brought him to tears, and he felt bound by grief in a way that he never had been by chains or handcuffs. All his mighty publicity boasts—"Nothing on Earth Can Hold HOUDINI a Prisoner!"—must have stung of mockery in the shadow of her death.

"My very Existence seems to have expired with her," he told his brother, in letters written on formal black-bordered mourning stationery. "I try and scheme ahead as in the Past, but I seem to have lost all ambition."

☞"Ma Saw Me Jump!"

Days before setting sail for Europe in the summer of 1913, Houdini hired a car and brought his mother and two of his brothers, Theo and Nat, to Cypress Hills Cemetery to visit the grave of his father, Mayer Samuel Weiss.

Houdini's competitive nature and deep love for his mother made for a complex relationship with his father, a brilliant man who had struggled to provide for the family. ("The less said on the subject the better," Houdini once wrote about the poverty and difficulty of his childhood.)

As an adult, he revered his father's memory, propping Mayer Samuel's portrait on his dressing-room table, but he admitted in diaries to feeling jealous and "insignificant" in his youth. He always wanted to be first—in Cecilia's affections as in all things—and competed with his father and five brothers and a sister for her attention.

Houdini's last promise to Mayer

Houdini had always loved Cecilia intensely—but not just because she was his mother. She was also his biggest and most important fan. The work he did, he did for her. The risks he took were for her also. "I am what would be called a Mothers-boy," he once confessed. "If I do anything, I say to myself I wonder if Ma would want me to do this?" Though Houdini was only thirty-nine years old—still at the heights of his professional power—his mother's absence was a kind of paralysis.

Trying to ease both mental and physical strain in his life, he dropped his escapes for a while and assembled an all-magic show, the "Grand Magical Revue," a project he enjoyed, though his promoters didn't. They argued that people wanted—and now expected from him—the big-ticket escapes he'd staked his reputation on.

After a weary year abroad, Houdini returned to New York in 1914 aboard the *Imperator*. His crossing from England, and a

Houdini kissing his "Sainted Mother," Cecilia, in Rochester, New York, 1908.

Samuel was that he would always care for his mother. His work often took him away from her, but he honored this vow above all, escorting Cecilia to his performances when he could and taking a special pride in risking his life for her. After the first of what would prove many high-risk manacled bridge jumps, in Rochester in 1907, he bragged in his diary, "Ma saw me jump!"

Rochester N.Y. 1908

performance he gave on board for a select audience, made US headlines, appearing alongside rumors of war in Europe.

In the audience at that performance was former president Theodore "Teddy" Roosevelt. (His preferred nickname was "the Colonel," a reference to military service preceding his term of office.) A great sportsman and adventurer, Roosevelt had recently returned from a wilderness expedition to map the Amazon rain forest's unexplored River of Doubt. When his prestigious fan requested a séance, Houdini cast back to his days as a fake medicine-show spirit medium. In a wild coincidence, Roosevelt happened to ask "the spirits" where he was the previous Christmas,

Houdini aboard the SS Imperator *with Theodore Roosevelt, 1914; fellow passengers have been airbrushed out of the picture.*

and Houdini happened to be able to produce a rigged spirit slate with a map of lower South America and the River of Doubt chalked on. "It was a shame the way I had to fool him," he recalled later.

The next morning on deck, the former president asked, "man to man," was the map produced by "genuine Spiritualism"?

"No, Colonel," Houdini admitted. "It was hokus pokus."

In a souvenir photo taken aboard ship, Houdini appears to be standing alone on deck with Roosevelt; in fact, Houdini airbrushed five other men out, leaving just himself and the Colonel. Ever the savvy self-promoter, he had his doctored portrait copyrighted, handing out many hundreds of publicity copies.

Back in New York, overwhelmed by memories, Houdini leased out the elegant Harlem brownstone that he and Bess had shared with Cecilia and other family members at intervals for the past ten years. "The Home is a Home no longer for me," he concluded, "and must be disposed of." He and Bess temporarily moved in with Theo's family in Brooklyn.

Theo was a magician, too, billed as Hardeen. Not surprisingly, the assertive Houdini (who had launched his little brother's career) expected top billing offstage as well as on, so living conditions must have felt a bit cramped for everyone.

Houdini continued to visit the gravesite in Queens often. Diary entries from the time prove that his grief was as raw as ever: "Here I am left alone on the station," he wrote in one, "bewildered and not knowing when the next train comes along *so that I can join my mother.*"

A few days after Houdini's return to the United States, the heir to the throne of the Austro-Hungarian Empire, Archduke Franz Ferdinand, and his wife were assassinated. In the coming months, Czar Nicholas II rallied his army, Germany invaded Belgium and declared war on France, and Britain declared war on Germany. With armies engaging along the western front—the main theater of war in France and Belgium—Houdini canceled his overseas bookings and agreed to play the Keith and Orpheum vaudeville houses throughout the United States instead.

His sixteen-month tour included stops in Boston, upstate New York, Canada, the Midwest, and elsewhere. In Kansas City, he debuted one of his most dangerous and spectacular stunts.

Over a period of three years after his mother's death, whenever he performed in a big city with skyscrapers, Houdini riveted audiences with his Suspended Straitjacket Escape. From the back of a horse-drawn wagon (usually parked at the curb near a major daily newspaper), he greeted the crowd through a megaphone, laughing and joking, waving his hat as fans waved theirs back.

Volunteers fitted his arms into the canvas or leather straitjacket, tying them over his chest, and then he lay flat while his ankles were bound. Finally he was hoisted up by crane—up and up, dangling head down, sometimes hundreds of feet in the air. While the masses craned their necks and murmured below, he began to squirm and twist and thrash, blood running to his face, the tendons in his neck swelling, until he had miraculously freed himself from the straitjacket and let it fall to earth.

A theatrical poster advertising Houdini's magician brother, Hardeen, 1931.

☞ I Want to Be First

In 1914, many Americans were still calling the nightmarish conflict across the Atlantic "Europe's war," but it was out there, looming large, and entertainment was a welcome distraction. Houdini brought a mind-boggling illusion back to New York with him that year called Walking Through a Brick Wall. He had a small army of masons construct a high wall right onstage; it ran from rear to front, so the audience could see both sides of the stage. With fanfare, and the usual committee culled from the crowd to assist and inspect his work, he appeared to pass right through the brick barrier to the other side of the stage.

He dropped the illusion, though, when another magician claimed ownership. Houdini couldn't bear to be copied—"puny attempts at duplication" enraged him—and the accusation called for swift action. He stopped performing Walking Through a Brick Wall and gave it over to his magician brother, Hardeen, the one professional imitator he didn't denounce (unless it made for good publicity). "I want to be first," Houdini told reporters, "first in my profession. . . . I have tortured my body and risked my life only for that."

Houdini suspended in a straitjacket at the Police Field Day Games at Gravesend Race Track in New York, August 29, 1920.

It was a dangerous stunt, one that over time killed several imitators. Houdini himself had, on past occasions, gashed his head on a window ledge in rough winds and hung stranded when a suspension crane jammed and ropes tangled. A window washer came to his rescue with a length of tied towels, luckily, before the pressure in his head did him in.

The master showman understood that he wasn't alone in his growing fascination with mortality and madness (the idea for the straitjacket escape struck during a visit to an insane asylum in Canada, one of his many asylum visits). "The easiest way to attract a crowd," he observed, "is to let it be known that at a given time and a given place some one is going to attempt something that in the event of failure will mean sudden death."

But within three years, exhausted from extreme emotional and physical stress, Houdini decided to "work entirely" with his brain. It was a timely decision; in 1916, movies were beginning to challenge vaudeville as the dominant form of popular entertainment, and many stage stars like Buster Keaton and Charlie Chaplin were making the leap to Hollywood—as would Houdini on and off.

Houdini's determination to work with his brain was more

JESSE L. LASKY
PRESENTS

HOUDINI
IN
"THE GRIM GAME"

BY ARTHUR B. REEVE AND JOHN W. GRAY
DIRECTED BY IRVIN WILLAT

A PARAMOUNT-ARTCRAFT PICTURE

Poster advertising Houdini's 1919 motion picture The Grim Game.

☞ Celluloid Detours

In 1916, wise to the growing popularity of photography and moving pictures, Houdini opened the Film Development Corporation, which offered high-speed film processing. At first, it seemed the West Hoboken, New Jersey, company would prosper, but Houdini wasn't a businessman, and the company failed financially.

He had only slightly more luck in front of the camera. His first starring role was in *The Master Mystery*, a cliff-hanger serial in fifteen episodes. *The Grim Game* (1919), *Terror Island* (1920), and others followed, but while fame assured Houdini an audience, his acting and range of expressions were limited. Opening his own movie studio to showcase his screen work didn't help matters. The physical power and presence of his escapes was diminished on-screen. Everyone knew movies were an "illusion," so his feats were just part of the mechanism.

than a reaction to the changing landscape of American entertainment. He was growing older; inevitably, his strength and physical power would fail him, and he would no longer be able to carry out the feats that had made him famous.

His intellectual ambition also echoed old feelings about his father. A respected scholar who toiled in obscurity and poverty, Rabbi Mayer Samuel had both let his family down (in material terms) and inspired their devotion. Houdini had craved his father's approval almost as much as his mother's love. At the same time, he blamed him for the lean and difficult years of his childhood and the shame that went with them.

Determined to be more than a showman and to honor his erudite father's memory, Houdini put together what he claimed was the world's largest collection, private or public, of material relating to magic and things mysterious. He traveled with a vast library and made the acquaintance of literary giants like Jack London and Rudyard Kipling. But his meeting with an especially influential man of letters would lead to one of the most surprising celebrity friendships of all time.

Bess Houdini with her husband's book collection, 1926.

FOUR

The Torch Bearer

"I do not say that I think, but I say that I KNOW that the dead live and come back to us. I have seen them. I have heard them. I have touched them. If I did not believe the evidence of my own senses I should not be sane." ~Sir Arthur Conan Doyle

The supremely logical detective Sherlock Holmes, one of the most popular literary characters ever, earned his creator fame and legions of adoring fans. But by the time Sir Arthur Conan Doyle met Houdini, in 1920, the author saw his beloved creation as a means to an end; the fictional detective was a ticket to "recognition, perhaps friendship, at the firesides throughout the world." Sherlock Holmes had paved Doyle's way as "the torch bearer of spiritualism."

With the First World War, Spiritualism had grown from earnest parlor games and theater in the dark to true religion. Doyle saw himself as a prophet of the faith, entrusted with a "new Revelation." Spiritualism was "the most important development in the whole history of the human race," he claimed, and it was his job to shout it from the rooftops.

🖝 Deception—or Consolation?

Popular belief in Spiritualism came and went after one of its founders, Maggie Fox, publicly denied the faith in 1888 (her sister Kate corroborated their fraud the same year), confessing that the rapping and phenomena she and her sisters had staged were a "horrible deception." This might have been the end, as she intended, "the death blow" for Spiritualism, but with the outbreak of World War I, belief swelled again. Eight million died in muddy trenches and on battlefields; and on the eve of peace—in the spring and summer of 1918, in an age before widespread vaccines—an influenza pandemic wiped out many millions more.

By 1920, nearly every person in England, for example, had lost someone dear. Newspapers and magazines on both sides of the Atlantic were full of reports—sincere, sensational, or otherwise—of psychic phenomena, and the spirit debate raged among scientists, ministers, magicians, and the ordinary public.

Red Cross emergency ambulance station in Washington, DC, during the influenza pandemic of 1918.

The man who had, in Sherlock Holmes, presented a genius of deductive reasoning wasn't the only educated convert to the idea of communication between the living and dead. In the 1920s, as in the late 1800s, many great minds were engaged in this issue.

Notable scientists subjected mediums to controlled investigations. Some, like the English chemist Sir William Crookes, a president of London's academy of science, the Royal Society, played an avid and active role. Others, intrigued or skeptical or both, joined organizations like the Society for Psychical Research (SPR).

Back in England honoring contracts he had made before the war, Houdini sent Sir Arthur Conan Doyle a copy of his book *The Unmasking of Robert-Houdin*, hoping to engage the author in friendly dialogue.

Doyle enjoyed the book, which touched on the history of magic; but he objected, in his reply, to Houdini's claim that the legendary Davenport brothers were not mediums but stage performers.

Normally outspoken in his opinions, Houdini held back. Doyle was too important (and possibly intimidating) a contact to alienate.

Sir Arthur Conan Doyle, circa 1900.

But as the correspondence continued, and Doyle's arguments in favor of the Davenport myth wore on, Houdini finally, diplomatically, replied: "I am afraid that I cannot say that all their work was accomplished by the spirits."

They exchanged about ten letters in two weeks. Houdini knew Spiritualism from the other side, a place of fakery and sleight of

Photo by White Studio.

PERFORMING AT THE HIPPODROME, NEW YORK.

*Houdini and Jennie the elephant performing at the
Hippodrome, New York, 1918.*

hand. Since his days as a fake medium, he hadn't given the whole
question much thought. But now, again, he did.

It may be that Doyle, the sort of legendary man of letters
Houdini aspired to be, stirred up his competitive pride. Houdini
was no slouch when it came to illusions and how they were con-
structed. He could make an elephant disappear, after all—and
had, onstage in New York's Hippodrome Theater, in 1918.

A "mystifier of mystifiers," he'd spent his life baffling audiences and his peers in the magic game. "I view these so-called
phenomena from a different angle than the ordinary layman or

even the expert investigator," he argued, and he knew how possible it was to conjure spirits for receptive eyes.

But in deference, and to smooth the way with Doyle, he held his tongue and played the role of willing convert. "I am seeking truth, and it is only by knowing that Analytical Minds are going in for it that I am treating this matter seriously."

Houdini was still in England playing the Brighton Hippodrome when Sir Arthur invited him to visit the Doyle family estate, Windlesham, in Sussex, where Houdini had lunch in their red-roofed gabled country house with Sir Arthur and Lady Doyle, Jean Leckie.

William James with a medium, circa 1910.

🖘 Strange Society

Founded in London in 1882, the Society for Psychical Research (SPR) was an elite membership of scholars and scientists—pioneers in psychology, psychiatry, physics, astronomy, and other disciplines—who investigated topics like ghost and poltergeist phenomena, extrasensory perception (ESP), and hypnosis. The only major organization at the time committed to studying paranormal activity and human consciousness, the society attracted the likes of Sir Arthur Conan Doyle, Sigmund Freud, and Carl Jung.

By 1885, an American Society for Psychical Research (ASPR) was formed, with pioneering psychologist and Harvard professor of philosophy William James serving as president from 1894 to 1895.

During the visit, Houdini performed tricks for what he saw as an unusually innocent (to deception) audience. He learned that Doyle believed he had conversed six times with his dead son and that Lady Doyle practiced trance writing, receiving messages from spirits through subconscious or "automatic" means. Houdini had his doubts on both counts but kept silent. He later described the visit in his diary. The couple's faith was unshakable, he observed. Spirit communication was a fact, and there was "no possible chance for trickery." Even hard evidence wouldn't sway them.

Houdini asked Doyle to recommend mediums, and Doyle agreed. He didn't expect Houdini to dispense with reason but simply to keep an open mind.

"My mind has always been open and receptive," Houdini insisted. But on the evidence, in private, he *didn't* believe.

"Something must come your way," Doyle assured, "if you really persevere and get it out of your mind that you should follow it as a terrier follows a rat."

Houdini swore to visit the mediums humbly and sincerely, without prejudice.

IN SPRING 1922, DOYLE AND HIS FAMILY CAME TO New York on a North American lecture tour of New York, Boston, Washington, DC, Philadelphia, Buffalo, Toronto, Detroit, Toledo, and Chicago. Sir Arthur gave several presentations at Carnegie Hall, at least one of which Houdini attended, though it would be three weeks before the friends met again one-on-one.

Sir Arthur's New York visit caused a sensation—with wildly mixed reviews.

A big, broad, plainspoken man in a double-breasted suit and gold spectacles, Doyle was no entertainer. He had come to New

York to spread the gospel of Spiritualism. But his talks reeled in some of the largest crowds Carnegie Hall had ever seen. On April 12, 1922, at the first of his six appearances, 3,500 people packed in, many claiming standing room. The hall hummed with women in mourning clothes, some with gold stars pinned on to show they had lost a loved one to the terrors of modern warfare: trenches and tanks, machine guns and poison gas.

According to some reports, Doyle commanded the room at once with his gravity and gentleness. His sturdy bulk, walrus mustache, and lilting Scots accent put people at ease, despite the eerie mood of the evening.

He told of parting with the Church while still a medical student, and of training as a doctor and eye specialist. But now, Doyle said, the skeptic was returned to wonder. He knew a little something about detective work, he joked, and this case was closed. He spoke of "the Etheric Body" and the afterlife, of the scientific evidence for survival.

He shared his own experiences: of making contact, "beyond any doubt," with his mother and other lost ones at séances. His son, Kingsley, a soldier wounded at the Battle of the Somme, had died of pneumonia in a London hospital right before peace was declared. Sir Arthur had heard again his dead son's voice through the channel of a spirit medium.

The *New York World* concluded: "In spite of the imagination of his writings, he seems to be a downright person. He does not look a man who could be easily stampeded. His audience was profoundly attentive. Evidently it was a crowd which had its dead."

Other reviews were harsh: could this believer in ghosts be the same man who gave the world the singularly rational Sherlock Holmes? Critics used words like "pathetic," even "senile."

These mean-spirited observations were a harsh echo of Houdini's own doubts, which would soon crack the surface of their friendship. Sir Arthur was a brilliant man, Houdini admitted, "a deep thinker, well versed in every respect." But his influence, Houdini feared, could mislead countless others, if that great brain were misled:

> *No statistician could fathom the influence [Sir Arthur Conan Doyle] has exerted through his lectures and his writings or number the endless chain he guides into a belief in communication with the Realm Beyond. . . . It is impossible not to respect the belief of this great author.*

During the tour, the Doyles invited the Houdinis to join them in Atlantic City, then a fashionable seaside resort, for a weekend getaway. "The children would teach you to swim," Doyle offered, and Harry and Bess (who wanted but were unable to have chil-

Sir Arthur Conan Doyle and his family in New York, April 1922.

dren) took a room next to the Doyles' suite in the Ambassador Hotel for two days in June.

Harry entertained the children with magic tricks and showed off how long he could stay submerged in the hotel swimming pool. Later, while the Doyles' three young ones splashed and played with a beach ball nearby, Houdini and the Doyles lounged in deck chairs and talked about Spiritualism and other topics of mutual interest.

On Sunday, while the Houdinis were enjoying a bit of

alone time on the beach, Doyle walked out with an invitation. Would Houdini like to join him and his wife in their suite for a private séance? Lady Doyle suspected a mediumistic message "might come through."

It's interesting that Bess was *not* invited. Sir Arthur apologized for not admitting Houdini's wife and closest confidant into the séance. Two people so alike in mind as Harry and Bess, he argued, might block incoming messages.

Did Sir Arthur worry the partners would unite in doubt and

☞ The Power Behind the Throne

Bess more or less retired from the stage early on to support her husband's ambitions; she and Houdini were far from equals professionally. But behind the scenes, they remained partners in every sense of the word. She was central to his work and life until (and even after) the end. They traveled everywhere together, sometimes employing Houdini's magical trunks to smuggle beloved pets in and out of unwelcoming countries. Bess rarely missed a performance, however dangerous and frightening for her. Houdini consulted her on all decisions, and she saw to everything from finances to his personal hygiene. (Left to his own devices, Harry got a bit slovenly; Bess did her best to keep him in line and looking sharp.)

Though loyal and supportive, willing to play second fiddle to the force of nature that was Houdini, Bess returned to the spotlight from time to time, usually to resurrect their classic Metamorphosis routine. In later years, she would characterize herself and other magicians' wives as "the power behind the throne" and resume a stage career of her own.

Bess Houdini, circa 1900.

undermine the gravity of the proceedings? Or did he just believe Houdini would be more receptive alone?

But in fact, Bess was no skeptic. She believed in ghosts; her superstitious nature even riled Houdini at times. The partners weren't, as Doyle assumed, automatically of one mind on this topic. Would the outcome (or the historical narrative) have been different had Bess attended?

Houdini hesitated, but curiosity won out in the end. He left Bess to her sunbathing and followed Sir Arthur back inside the Ambassador.

With the hotel blinds drawn to close out the bright ocean sunlight, and writing pads and pencils on the table, he sat beside Lady Doyle as Sir Arthur bowed his head and uttered a prayer, calling for a sign from "our friends from beyond." Doyle then covered his wife's hands with his own. Was she ready?

Lady Doyle withdrew one shaking hand and struck the table three times. Houdini, meanwhile, cleared his mind of all but "religious" thoughts. "I made up my mind," he wrote later, "that I would . . . [give] my whole soul to the séance. I was willing to believe, even *wanted* to believe. It was weird to me and with a beating heart I waited, hoping that I might feel once more the presence of my beloved Mother."

Houdini did, in fact, believe in an afterlife—as had his rabbi father. What he didn't believe was that the dead had reason or opportunity to reach back to the living. But he could still hope. And today he did.

Breathing hard, Lady Doyle lifted a pencil. Her eyelids fluttered, and she quaked all over. Soon her hand began to fly across the notebook page as if on its own, jerking with tremendous energy, the other thumping the table as she scrawled strings of tall, disconnected letters.

Houdini later claimed that the message ran fives pages; Sir Arthur, fifteen. But it was clearly meant to be from Cecilia Weiss,

Houdini's mother: "Oh my darling, thank God, thank God, at last I am through. I've tried, oh so often—now I am happy. Why, of course, I want to talk to my boy—my own beloved boy—friends, thank you, with all my heart for this. . . ."

She was happy, she assured him. They would be reunited one day. It was different where she was: "nothing that hurts."

"I have bridged the gulf," the script said. "That is what I wanted, oh so much—now I can rest in peace."

Doyle sat opposite, tearing sheets from the notebook as they filled up, "tossing each to Houdini," who "sat silent, looking grimmer and paler at every moment." Doyle reported later that Houdini left the séance "deeply moved."

In fact, Houdini was fuming.

For starters, Lady Doyle had marked a Christian cross on each page of her pad. His mother was a rabbi's wife. She would never have communicated with a cross. Second, Cecilia Weiss did not read, write, or speak more than broken English. She would have written in German or one of several other European languages she knew (though the Doyles would argue that spirits communicate in the native language of the medium; what's more, psychics like Etta Wriedt, who spoke only English, could apparently channel spirit messages in French, German, Italian, Spanish, Norwegian, Dutch, Arabic, and other languages). Third, the day of the séance, June 17, was his mother's birthday. Houdini felt she would have mentioned this.

He "did not have the nerve" to challenge—or let down?—Sir Arthur, and held his disappointment in check. But Houdini brooded over the séance, and within months it would spell the end of their friendship.

Houdini's doubts were pooling into conviction.

Good, honest, educated people—people longing to believe in a life after this one and to hear from their dead—had "surrendered themselves to belief in the most monstrous fiction."

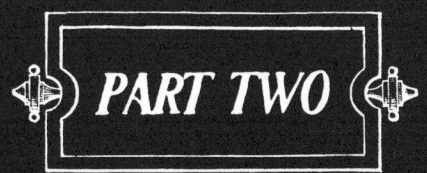

PART TWO

Methods and Madness

FIVE

"In the Light"

*"Some persons think the requirement of
darkness seems to [imply] trickery. Is not
a dark chamber essential in the process of
photography? And what would we reply to
him who would say, 'I believe photography
to be a humbug—do it all in the light, and we
will believe otherwise'?"* ~Dion Boucicault,

IN DEFENSE OF THE DAVENPORT BROTHERS

D uring Sir Arthur's Carnegie Hall lectures, a deep hush
fell over the auditorium when he dimmed the lights and
began to project images on the screen by stereopticon.

Spirit photographs, he told his packed houses at Carnegie Hall,
were proof of the dead in our presence.

"The darkness of the theater," the *New York Herald* reported
later, "the spookiness, the uncanny effects produced by the pictures and the impressive sincerity of Sir Arthur as he told the
history of the subject on the screen had a weird effect upon the
crowd."

Doyle's presentations featured pictures by William Mumler,
a Boston jewelry engraver and amateur photographer who had
made a name for himself decades earlier.

Harper's Monthly *from May 8, 1869, featuring an article about the trial of William Mumler.*

One March day in 1861, Mumler took an experimental self-portrait and developed the photographic plate, astonished to find a ghostly female face near his. He'd double exposed the image, imprinting or layering one image over another on a single plate of film. But with Spiritualism at its peak, and "being of a jovial disposition, always ready for a joke," Mumler shared the mysterious self-portrait (plus extra) with a devout Spiritualist he knew, Dr. H. F. Gardner, who saw there a miracle.

Gardner put the image out on the Spiritualist wire with a statement from the photographer: "This photograph was taken of myself, by myself, on Sunday, when there was not a living soul in the room besides me—'so to speak.' The form on my right I recognize as my cousin who passed away about twelve years since." A bewildered Mumler soon found himself a "humble instrument in the hands of the invisible host that surrounds us." Like the "rapping" phenomena of the Fox sisters thirteen years earlier, what began as a harmless joke quickly assumed a life of its own.

Convinced the photographer was channeling the dead,

Spirit photograph with "extras," 1901.

☞ How to Shoot Spirits

Spirit photography can be created on-camera or in a darkroom using basic techniques like double exposure (exposing the same frame of film twice), sandwiching glass or film negatives together during the printing stage, or (today) digitally manipulating the image.

Houdini notes other methods in his book *A Magician Among the Spirits,* from the complicated—piercing a negative with X-rays in the developing stage—to the very simple: removing the lens cap and, with a bit of sleight of hand, holding a concealed object over the lens and blurring the focus. Snap a photo in secret before you take the "regular" exposure, and you've planted an "additional hazy something" on the sensitized plate.

You may ask, how did pictures like this fool anyone? Keep in mind that photographic science was still new and mysterious, and a "willing" public had little cause not to trust their own eyes.

believers came in droves. He quit his day job and, for a round fee, churned out portrait after portrait with dearly departed relatives or celebrities hovering mistily in the frame.

Controversy swirled around him. Prominent Bostonians who believed Mumler had re-united them, on film, with lost loved ones sang his praises, but one skeptic predicted, in the *American Journal of Photography*, that spirit photography would soon be exposed as a "low swindle."

In fact, it was Dr. Gardner, the very man who had presented Mumler to Boston

Undated postmortem photo of a father and child.

☞ Postmortem Photography

Almost as soon as the new technology of photography became widely available to the public in the early nineteenth century, people used it to record the dead. Today the idea of flipping through pictures of dead people is unnerving, but at the same time we take pictures—print, electronic, animated—for granted. We're surrounded by them.

Kodak gave regular families access to snapshots in the 1890s, but before that, if you had no artist in the family, and no money to hire a portrait painter, you could end up without a single likeness of a person you held dear. The idea that somebody you loved was gone—forever, and you with no way to remember—must have been beyond difficult.

In many deathbed portraits, subjects appear to be sleeping peacefully, though a telltale rose or lily with a snapped stem in their grasp might hint otherwise.

society as a powerful link to the spirit world, who first accused the photographer of fraud. Gardner was shocked to discover, after an 1863 sitting with Mumler, that the ghostly likeness in the picture with him was no ghost at all. Mumler was "palming off, as genuine spirit likenesses, pictures of a person who is now living in this city," a woman who had visited the studio weeks before. When Gardner stepped up, other clients surfaced with complaints, and Mumler's reputation in Boston collapsed in a heap, forcing him to resume work as a jewelry engraver.

In November 1868, determined to get back to work as a spirit photographer, he moved his family to New York City and took a job with the William W. Silver Gallery. Some five months and five hundred spirit photographs later, he was successful enough to buy out Silver's business. But the shop had scarcely changed hands when he was arrested and jailed for fraud.

A sensational trial followed in April and May, one that echoed the larger debate between believers and skeptics, science and faith, and put Spiritualism on the witness stand along with Mumler.

The prosecutor argued, "Man is naturally both credulous and superstitious, and in all ages of the world imposters and cheats have taken advantage."

He listed numerous ways spirit photographs might be faked, though no one seemed quite sure what Mumler's exact methods were. One thing was clear: spirit "extras" were less likely to turn up when those methods were under scrutiny. One esteemed portrait photographer testified that he saw no foul play in Mumler's technique, but most experts backed the prosecution: ghostly effects were easily achieved through earthly means. One boasted that he could photograph "a man with an angel over his head, or with a pair of horns on his head, just as I wish."

P. T. Barnum, 1855.

The prosecution also called to the stand master showman P. T. Barnum, who had blasted spirit photography in his 1866 book, *The Humbugs of the World: An Account of Humbugs, Delusions, Impositions, Quackeries, Deceits and Deceivers Generally, in All Ages*, but Mumler's lawyer challenged his testimony. Why was Mumler on trial when Barnum wasn't? His museum had been known to feature, just for starters, a dried mermaid. "Have you never . . . taken money for the exhibition of spurious curiosities?" the lawyer asked.

"I think," Barnum said, as the courtroom roared with laughter, "I *may* have given a little drapery with it sometimes."

The defense, for its part, mainly called Mumler's satisfied clients, including a state senator and a former US justice, sitters convinced that he had given them precisely what they came for.

"Persons of all classes, professions, and shades of opinion were present" at Mumler's trial, reported the *New York World*. The crowd was one of "the most intelligent that ever assembled in a New York police court," with "journalists, lawyers mighty in criminal proceedings, authors, physicians, artists, sculptors . . . all deeply interested in the solution of a question which they believe can only be answered by one of two alternatives—'A fraud' or 'A miracle.'"

Mumler himself insisted that he didn't know—had never claimed to know—how spirits were managing to show up and have their portraits taken. Charged with deciding whether felony and misdemeanor charges should be presented to the grand jury, Judge John Dowling was "morally" certain Mumler's clients had been tricked, but since no one had actually caught the photographer red-handed, or proved deceit in his methods, the justice was obliged to let him go.

But Mumler's reputation moved with him, and though he set up shop again in Boston and continued to take portraits—including a famous view of widow Mary Todd Lincoln being comforted by her spirit husband, the assassinated President Lincoln—his tarnished career never fully recovered.

In 1875, a few years after the Mumler trial, an artful French medium and photographer named Édouard Isidore Buguet was similarly arrested and charged. When police seized the contents of Buguet's studio as evidence, they

William Mumler photograph of Mary Todd Lincoln with the "ghost" of her husband.

found a stash of life-size doll heads: the model for spirit "extras." After admitting in court that he double exposed for his effects, he was convicted and sentenced to a year in jail and a fine of five hundred francs.

☞ Airy Images

Magicians, too, used ghostly pictures to amaze their public. At phantasmagoria shows, illusionists projected pictures on a waxed screen, toying with the focus and using hidden lanterns to change the size and shape of the spectral figures they projected. These "air images," as handbills and ads called them, often featured celebrities—living and dead—like Napoléon Bonaparte.

Robertson's phantasmagoria, Paris, 1797.

What's interesting about Buguet's case is that some of his clients—educated people from all walks of life who had sat for the photographer and received spirit portraits of loved ones—refused to accept his guilt or surrender their faith, *even after* Buguet explained the mechanics of his deception.

A police officer testified that Buguet had shown off the portrait of a woman who'd served as the spirit sister of one sitter, the mother of another, and the friend of a third. Buguet even

showed how he had used the image of a live subject who proved "much annoyed at his premature introduction to the Spirit world."

Spirit photography faded out for a time but reemerged, alongside demand for other spirit manifestations, in England especially, in the wake of the war and pandemic.

In the 1910s and '20s, medium William Hope and his famous Crewe Circle perfected the technique of adding "extras" to unexposed film. Like Mumler and Buguet before him, Hope gained a following and attracted controversy.

Along with Mumler's, Hope's projected images had made a stir during Sir Arthur Conan Doyle's Carnegie Hall lectures.

Doyle told of visiting Hope and his medium, Mrs. Buxton, in

Spirit photograph by Édouard Isidore Buguet, circa 1873.

Spirit photograph by William Hope, 1920.

1918, after his son Kingsley's death, and again in the summer of 1919. At his third Hope séance, he got an image of his son. The audience let out a collective gasp when Doyle projected on the screen the slide of misty Kingsley staring tenderly at his father.

The spirit was not "a very good likeness," Doyle confessed to the rapt crowd at Carnegie Hall—too youthful—but he added, "You may realize how consoling it was to me, in any circumstances, to see my son again."

In December 1921—busy making his own skeptical inquiries in light of his ongoing debate with Sir Arthur—Houdini tried to call on Hope and have his picture taken with a spirit. He was told the photographer's engagements "would keep him busy for months."

The Curious Case of the Vanishing Lion

On February 24, 1922, not long after William Hope and his Crewe Circle set up shop in London, Harry Price and a fellow investigator went undercover to Hope's studio at the British College of Psychic Science. Their task was to commission spirit portraits for inspection without letting on who they were.

By then it was common practice to bring your own photographic plates (in a lightproof plate holder) for the medium to "magnetize" (this was how photographers assured sitters that no tricks were involved in the processing stage). Price had marked his plates beforehand—using X-rays—with a lion emblem, invisible to the naked eye. When Hope's séance with Price wrapped up, a spirit image had manifested on the plate, but close inspection showed no lion. The SPR accused Hope of switching the plates and plate holders.

Later the same year, Price published his findings, outing Hope as a fraud. But faithful followers stuck by him, including Sir Arthur Conan Doyle, who wrote a book called *The Case for Spirit Photography* in his defense.

Hope uniformly refused to submit his methods to scientific scrutiny, but an undercover sting by the SPR would soon expose him.

Disillusionments aside, Doyle continued to support the photographer and his circle, and Hope stayed in business until he died in 1933.

One of the last images Doyle projected on the screen during his Carnegie Hall lectures was a photograph taken by medium and former cleaning lady Ada Emma Deane. Doyle introduced it as "the greatest spirit photo ever taken."

Taken at a memorial ceremony on November 11, 1922, in London's Whitehall during

☞ Fairies on Film

With the 1922 publication of his book *The Coming of the Fairies*, Sir Arthur endangered his already reduced credibility by championing photographs taken by young Elsie Wright and her cousin Frances, two girls who claimed to play with fairies in their Cottingley garden in rural Yorkshire, England. To Doyle, "proving the existence of fairies" meant "opening the way to a new world," and the controversy spanned decades, even after his death.

In 1983, when she was seventy-six years old, Frances finally confessed that the fairies had been traced from *Princess Mary's Gift Book*, cut out, pasted on cards, and positioned with hat pins.

"Among all the notable persons attracted to Spiritualism," psychic investigator Harry Price said of Doyle, "he was perhaps the most uncritical. His extreme credulity, indeed, was the despair of his colleagues, all of whom, however, held him in the highest respect for his complete honesty."

Elsie Wright's photograph "Alice and the Fairies," July 1917.

A. ALICE AND THE FAIRIES.
Copyright. Photograph taken July, 1917.

two minutes of silent prayer for Britain's war dead, the image showed the sky over the Armistice crowd swarming with the faces of young men killed in battle . . . milky, lost, neckless heads with shocked eyes and furrowed brows.

According to the *New York Times*, when the picture filled the screen in Carnegie Hall, the whole house gasped. A number of women sobbed violently, and Doyle had to pause the presentation while they were comforted.

It later came out that the disembodied faces in the sky belonged to thirteen soccer and boxing celebrities, all alive and well. The greatest spirit photograph ever taken turned out to be a great big hoax, and the joke was on Sir Arthur. (Unfortunately, the image hasn't aged well.)

"From a logical, rational point of view," said Houdini—though he wouldn't have been able to convince Sir Arthur, who, not surprisingly, defended Ada Deane even after she was exposed—"spirit photography is a most barefaced imposition . . . evidence of how unscrupulous mediums become and how calloused their consciences."

☞ The Even More Curious Case of the Reappearing Lion

On March 3, 1922, a week after the Price investigation into Hope and the Crewe Circle, a wrapped photographic plate arrived in the mail at the SPR offices. The mystery plate, once developed, revealed the distinct imprint of both a ghost and a lion.

An SPR "counter" committee, including society member Sir Arthur Conan Doyle, concluded that Price had been bamboozled, along with Hope, by a furtive enemy of mediums and psychic science out to sabotage the proceedings.

These allegations prompted Doyle to quit the SPR the following year.

The proof was plain, he argued, in what would soon become a standard mode of attack for him: "For upwards of forty years there have been standing offers of money in the amounts ranging from five hundred to five thousand dollars for a single case of so-called phenomena which could be proven actually psychic." No spirit photographer had ever volunteered. "If there are any who are operating honestly," Houdini challenged, "let them come forward with proof and take the reward."

A portrait of psychic investigator Harry Price, inscribed to Houdini, 1921.

"Poor, dear, loveable, *credulous Doyle. He was a giant in stature with the heart of a child.*"

—HARRY PRICE, PSYCHIC INVESTIGATOR

SIX

Manifestations!

"Strange how people imagine things in the dark! Why, the musical instruments never left our hands yet many spectators would have taken an oath that they heard them flying over their heads." ~Ira Davenport

Back when Houdini first arranged to visit spirit mediums on Sir Arthur's recommendation, his first stop was a Mrs. Anna Brittain. "The best," Doyle claimed.

Brittain's best effort—talking a lot and in generalities—didn't impress Houdini one whit. "This is ridiculous stuff," the magician reported in his diary.

Mediums claim to contact the dead through psychic or paranormal means, and the means vary: some psychics are clairvoyant and work visually; others are clairsentient or clairaudient and rely on their intuition or hearing. Some channel, summon, or "materialize" spirits.

Houdini next sat for a séance with Mrs. Wriedt, a medium known for attracting spirit voices.

That, too, was a bust. His dead were dead silent.

"She was afraid of me," Houdini guessed, and in fact, the

medium later informed Sir Arthur that the magician was "out to make trouble."

"I never look for trouble," was the not-so-innocent reply.

Sir and Lady Doyle hosted Wriedt at their estate a few days later with contrasting success: as the Doyles, a friend, and the séance medium sang together at a table in the children's nursery, a fifth, "very beautiful" voice joined in, distinct from Mrs. Wriedt's. "Now, is not that quite final?" challenged Doyle.

Whether Houdini went looking for trouble or not, he found it. "You have a reputation among Spiritualists of being a bitterly prejudiced enemy," Doyle assured him.

Some mediums refused to sit for him at all.

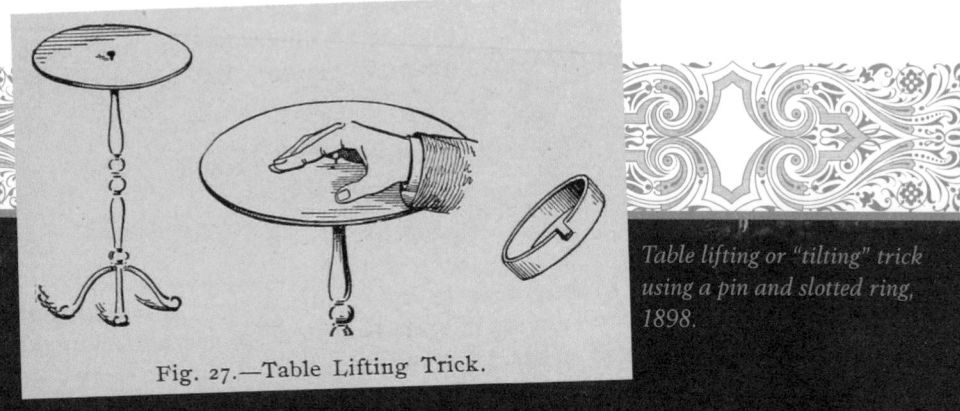

Fig. 27.—Table Lifting Trick.

Table lifting or "tilting" trick using a pin and slotted ring, 1898.

☞ Spectral Rock and Roll

Table tipping, like the popular Ouija board or planchette, was all the rage at "home circles" or séances in the nineteenth century. Participants laid their hands lightly on a special three-legged table, fingertips touching, while someone posed a question. As "spirit" energy surged through their hands, the table would vibrate, tip, "gallop," or rap out a coded reply (all easy phenomena to fake, according to Houdini).

Chemist and physicist Michael Faraday threw cold water on the Victorian fad for table tipping. His experiment proved that even earnest (non-faked) rocking and rolling was the result of the involuntary muscle contractions of the living, a case of collective unconscious at work, not a visitation from the dead.

To "get truth in the matter," said Doyle, "you must submit in a humble spirit."

Whether Houdini accepted the fact or not, the ball was emphatically in the other court. The "forces beyond," his friend warned, "are repelled by frivolity or curiosity but act under the impulse of sympathy."

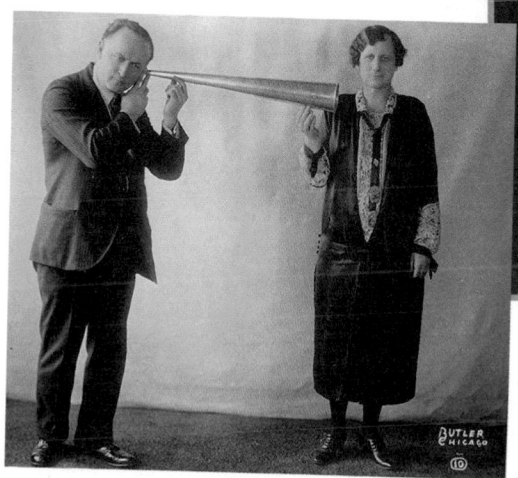

One medium whom Houdini was eager to observe was the mysterious and much-discussed Eva Carrière or "Eva C." from France.

When mediums entered altered states of consciousness, they claimed spirits communicated through their voices, gestures, features, or bodies. By far one of the strangest techniques that mediums worked with, and a fashionable one in the 1920s—in the way that "rapping" was fashionable in the time of the Fox sisters—was to enter a trance and produce a substance called ectoplasm. Supposedly created from a spirit's energy field, ectoplasm was

The medium Eva C., 1912.

sticky, glutinous, unsavory-looking stuff that issued from a medium's nose, ears, and other orifices. Thought to be a spirit's consciousness or emotion given form, it often assumed the shape of human limbs and faces.

Ectoplasm, which had to be made in near darkness (mediums claimed it dissolved in the light), was Eva C.'s specialty.

Houdini managed to get a sitting with the medium but had to work hard for it.

☞ Psychic Show-and-Tell

Mental mediumship, it's said, occurs within a psychic's consciousness. Through mental telepathy (thought transference), the medium sees, hears, or feels what a spirit communicator—a "control" or "guide"—wants to share. The content is subjective. It's up to the sitter to recognize or interpret whatever message is delivered. Spirit communicators have plenty to *say*, speaking through the channel of a medium, but nothing to *show*.

Physical mediums, on the other hand, work in league with spirit "operators" to *demonstrate* spirit presence. In near darkness, with help from this select breed of medium, the spirit makes or manifests something: ectoplasm, phantom hands, spectral music, orbs of light. Raps echo over walls. A planchette glides across a Ouija board. The operator from Beyond might even cause objects—or the medium herself—to levitate. These alleged phenomena are objective, witnessed by everyone present at a séance.

Like many Spiritualists, Eva C.'s handler, Madame Juliette Bisson, believed that magicians were biased against psychic phenomena. She didn't trust them. Houdini won Bisson over by inviting the pair to a performance of the Water-Torture Cell Escape. The illusion so baffled and impressed Bisson and Eva C. that they asked to attend a second performance, and extended the invitation Houdini was after. "You are a magnificent actor," Bisson said, "who cannot call himself a prestidigitator [magician], a title beneath a man of your talent."

Houdini sat in on several

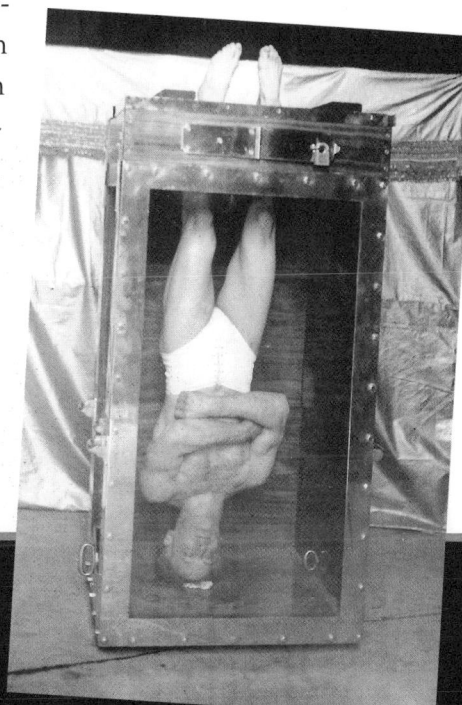

Houdini upside-down in the Water Torture Cell, circa 1912.

☛ **Water-Torture Cell Escape**

It took Houdini three years to plan one of his most thrilling and mystifying stage illusions—and it cost over ten thousand dollars. Built by British carpenter James Collins, the tall glass box might have been a phone booth or a standing glass coffin. Houdini debuted the escape, "the greatest sensational mystery ever attempted in this or any age," in 1912, at the Circus Busch in Berlin, to an audience gripped by the eerie sight of Houdini submerged, headfirst, in the locked box, his hair floating like anemones, his white hands groping the glass— to orchestra strains of "Asleep in the Deep."

With an assistant stationed nearby with an ax, set to smash the glass in an emergency, volunteers drew the curtain round. A massive stopwatch began to tick over the cell, and like Houdini, audiences must have held their collective breath. He emerged, drenched and gasping, with the cell still locked behind him, the floor still dry.

three-hour séances with Bisson and Eva C. held by the Society for Psychical Research. He refrained from "scoffing" and went in with "the will to believe" but with eyes wide open, "taking in even the most minute details and keeping on my guard against any trickery."

Several times, Houdini sat in the "control" chair beside the

Houdini demonstrating the Needle-Swallowing Trick, circa 1915.

☞ Eating Needles on a String

Houdini perplexed audiences (even doctors) for twenty-five years with his "East Indian" or "Hindoo" Needle-Swallowing Trick, an illusion he introduced in 1899. As he often did, he brought up members of the audience, a "committee" to rule out fraud, and had them peer up his nose and into his throat. He then asked them to watch carefully as he stuffed his mouth with sewing needles, chewing and crunching and joking all the while about "taking iron for the blood." One paper reported, "You can hear the steel crush and snap under his iron teeth." He then took a length of white thread and swallowed it, leaving just the end visible in his throat. At last he opened his mouth and let the committee shine a light in to confirm that his mouth was empty, before slowly, slowly reeling out a long string of threaded needles.

With his pacing and showmanship, Houdini made this trick look new and dangerous, but it was actually nearly a hundred years old, an illusion even amateur magicians can perform.

medium for the best vantage point. Eva C. was first searched by "lady members of the Committee" in the next room, after which Madame Bisson put her into "a mesmeric sleep" and the party would wait, often for hours.

At a séance in London on June 22, 1920, Eva C. "expelled from her mouth a great deal of foam," which began "adhering to her veil on the inside." Houdini suspected that her ectoplasm was in fact regurgitation, that Eva C. had worked some substance to her mouth by sleight of hand and then expelled it, a move "almost identical," he said, to "the manner in which I manipulate my [Needle-Swallowing] experiment."

Houdini decided that Bisson was "a subtle and gifted assistant to Eva." He didn't believe her "to be honest," and sensed something "wrong in the air" at the June 24 séance. In fact, the hosts, feeling mocked by another participant's comment, took offense and broke up the gathering.

Too often, Houdini found, mediums imposed fixed conditions on investigators to avoid scrutiny. When faced with exposure, they found some excuse to postpone or end a séance.

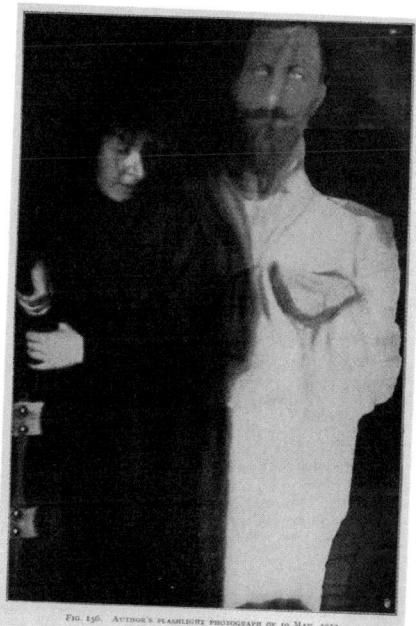

How could observers get the facts if the house rules were fixed; if séances resulted "in a blank" whenever mediums detected suspicion (and blamed investigators for bringing in "an atmosphere of incredulity" hostile to manifestations)?

It was hard enough that mediums insisted on darkness or near darkness. Sir Arthur argued, "If

Investigators discovered the figures appearing in Eva C.'s ectoplasm, like this example from 1913, were magazine cutouts.

you want to send a telegram you must go to a telegraph office," but to Houdini's mind, the condition of darkness was just another way that mediums kept clients in the dark, in more ways than one.

In the end, he didn't doubt that Bisson and Eva C. "simply took advantage of the credulity and good nature" of investigators. Houdini was sure they would be "authentically classified as questionable," and during fifteen séances in Paris, scientists at the Sorbonne confirmed that Eva C.'s manifestations showed "nothing beyond the simple act of regurgitation."

The *London Telegraph* reported that the "whiteness supposed to have come from the 'world beyond' was nothing but a Communicant's veil rolled up in the medium's pocket." Investigations by the Society for Psychical Research in London and an analysis of her ectoplasm revealed it to be made of chewed paper.

And the ghostly faces that sometimes appeared in that ectoplasm? Celebrity shots of Woodrow Wilson, King Ferdinand of Bulgaria, and French president Raymond Poincaré clipped from back issues of the French magazine *Le Miroir*.

Fired up now, Houdini sat with other mediums—some hun-

🖘 Spirit Wordsmiths

Many spirits had literary aspirations. The fifteen (or five, if you believe Houdini) pages that the Doyles transcribed for Houdini from his dead mother during the Atlantic City séance are a fraction of the spectral output. The writer Thomas Mann attended a séance in Berlin where a typewriter clacked away of its own volition with the medium nowhere near. "Any mechanical deception or sleight-of-hand tricks," Mann reported, "were humanly impossible." The spirits of scribes and statesmen like Shakespeare and Lincoln often waxed eloquent at séances.

And spirits passed on good wishes and warnings to loved ones through Spiritualist newspapers like Boston's *Banner of Light*, which kept a resident medium on staff and published what came through on a special mes-

dred or so, he claimed, over six months in Great Britain, with a stint in Paris—but still he held back his thoughts and findings out of deference to Sir Arthur. "He treats Spiritualism as a religion," Houdini complained later. "In his own mind, they are all genuine. Even if they are caught cheating he always has some sort of an alibi which excuses the medium and the deed."

Even if what Eva C. had on offer was not fraud—and Houdini was sure it was—he couldn't help but wonder what the so-called material evidence presented at séances could possibly add to human understanding of "the future state of a soul."

The manipulation of "horrible, revolting, viscous substances" and the appearance of "hideous shapes, which, like 'genii from the bronze bottle,' ring bells, move handkerchiefs, wobble tables, and do other 'flap-doodle' stunts," seemed to him not only deceptive but absurd.

HOUDINI STILL HADN'T REVEALED HIS TRUE FEEL-ings to Sir Arthur about Lady Doyle's message from his mother,

sage page. The contents of *The Spirit Messenger* and *Star of Truth*, both published in 1852, were said to be written and edited *by* spirits. In Spiritualist camps and communities like Lily Dale, in western New York, mediums served spirits by relaying messages to the pilgrims who showed up seeking consolation or communion with their dead.

and he continued to fume and investigate independently. He formally "began a new line of psychical research," assembling his findings for a lecture series and book on the subject.

If there was any "reality to the return, by Spirit, of one who had passed over the border," he would find it and devote "heart and soul and what brain power I possess" to the problem.

Reflecting on the kind of bald deception he saw in Eva C., Houdini again regretted "trifling with the hallowed reverence which the average human being bestows on the departed" when he had been a fake medium with the medicine show. At the time, he saw his skill for deception as play, a tool of his professional repertoire—like handcuffs and straitjackets. But the Atlantic City séance and the painful memories it stirred up had deepened his long-standing preoccupation with mortality and death.

With the years, he learned to identify with the bereaved who attended séances. "I too would have parted gladly with a large share of my earthly possessions for the solace of one word," he admitted—one word "genuinely bestowed."

Losing his mother didn't launch his escalating crusade to expose charlatans. But her "visitation" a decade later, and his renewed pain in light of the Doyles' séance, revealed to him the power that fake mediums held in the lives of grieving people. For the first time, the showman who had taken that power lightly "realized that it bordered on crime."

Houdini vowed never to step into "a séance room except with an open mind." The trouble was, he knew quite a few of the tricks physical mediums used to achieve their effects. It was hard to stay impartial when logic told him there was a material explanation for phenomena billed as psychic.

He knew that to make a spirit "rap" on a séance table, all you had to do, in the dark, was lift a leg and deftly knock the knee bone against the underside of the table, or fasten a wooden block beside the knee in advance and strike the wood sideways against a table leg. These and other methods took skill and practice but were by no means difficult.

One of Spiritualism's founders, Maggie Fox, had exposed her method for rapping (cracking her toe joints) decades ago, and Houdini had even observed a phenomenon where clients at séances contributed "involuntary and subconscious" table rapping and tapping, perhaps to spice up dreary proceedings.

"**I have attended** *séances where I have caught some one obligingly cheating to relieve the monotony.*"

—HOUDINI

Making tables levitate, another staple in spirit circles, was easily accomplished with help from a confederate, an assistant secretly planted in a séance.

Confederates, in fact, came in handy for all manner of phenomena.

Many magicians relied on secret codes for psychic mind-reading acts, as Houdini and Bess had early on; mediums and their confederates employed these methods, too, using clever silent codes or gestures to communicate their intentions to each other.

Once, while he was touring England, Houdini himself had given a dark séance where "just at the psychological moment a Spirit came through the window and walked around on the wall and ceiling of the room. . . . On the bill with me," he explained, "were two acrobats."

Sometimes, when a wealthy patron or an influential reviewer

A lantern slide of a séance featuring musical instruments, circa 1926.

was attending, *everyone* at a séance was a confederate except the "mark."

When the circle linked hands (as much to reassure the mark that the medium wasn't up to no good as to pool the group's energies and attract spirits), a common trick was for three confederates to sit together. This freed up the one in the middle to roam around the dark room and produce phenomena.

Even without confederates, savvy mediums could put on a show by smuggling in gadgetry. They concealed flat packets of clothing in their undergarments—"preferably cobweb-fine French muslin" brightened in spots with luminous oil made from phosphorus—or, since clothing was often searched beforehand, wore boots with hollow heels for storing supplies.

When a séance attended by investigators required participants to link hands *and* overlap feet (to ensure no escape-artist tricks on the part of the medium), some wore hard-toed boots that allowed them to deftly slip out a foot or feet, using these extremities and the strength of their legs to tip tables or thump out noises.

One female medium used a clever wire dummy coated with a fine skin of rubber, inflating it during a dark séance to look like the spirit form of a child. When it was deflated, the medium could fold it back up and wear it as a bustle neatly hidden under her skirts.

Some mediums wore special rings to correspond to a pin in the center of séance tables; hooking the ring there allowed them to manipulate the table.

Not surprisingly, Spiritualist performers preferred to host séances in the comfort of their homes. In one medium's house, investigators found a trapdoor beneath a cabinet. It opened into a passage leading to a back room, and *that* room contained a trapdoor out of the building.

WHEN HE COLLECTED HIS RESEARCH IN THE BOOK *A Magician Among the Spirits,* Houdini would devote a good dozen pages to the ingenious ways in which mediums collected information about their clients. Their campaigns were often planned far in advance of a séance and involved everything from blackmail and bribery (one young man, "greatly in debt," was compelled to take a job in the Bureau of Records and "furnish the medium with copies of certain documents") to arranging to have accomplices hired as domestic servants and chauffeurs in the homes of wealthy families. "If it is possible to steal the records of great political parties," Houdini argued, "how much easier to steal the secret papers of a family."

Mediums would hire confederates to troll "the 'gilded lobster palaces' of Broadway," hotel cabarets, Turkish baths, and so on, and get their victims drunk to gain their confidence or to rifle through their clothing for telltale letters or documents.

Houdini speaks of mediums hiring "a quiet couple for the express purpose of attending funerals, mixing with the mourners, and gathering information." The culprits would "dress some little woman demurely and place her in the reception room where she greets the visitors, telling them her troubles and naturally receiving confidences in return." He even recounts the tale of

☞ How Fake Mediums Obtain Information

To get the skinny on their clients, fakes in Houdini's day would:

- ✿ postpone séances to buy time and dig up dirt
- ✿ scan death, birth, engagement, and marriage notices in newspapers
- ✿ employ young men to mingle discreetly with guests at social events
- ✿ make trips on steamers to collect morsels of scandal in smoking and card rooms
- ✿ review court records of property and mortgages
- ✿ tap telephone wires
- ✿ plant assistants as waiters in restaurants, as well as business and luncheon clubs
- ✿ plant clerks in metropolitan hotels to open, read, and return guests' letters
- ✿ hire switchboard operators to intercept messages and transcribe conversations
- ✿ bribe servants, building superintendents, and elevator operators to make daily reports
- ✿ employ pickpockets to secure letters and business documents
- ✿ work for a time as traveling salesmen or fake census takers

"an old-time circus grafter who, having been cleaned out in Wall Street . . . invested what little capital he had and all he could borrow in a beauty parlor." The grafter took what he learned there and set himself up as a medium, "the venture yielding handsomely the first year."

The fact was, people told things about themselves without being remotely aware they were doing it. "Under the excitement of the moment their subconscious mind speaks," as Houdini put it, "while their conscious mind forgets. This does not escape the medium."

Outrageous though some of these methods sound, when there was money to be made, Houdini believed, fake mediums (he called them "human wolves," "human leeches," and "human vultures") would stop at nothing. Those "resourceful in obtaining information have made millions of dollars," he asserted, "blood money made at the cost of torture to the souls of their victims."

A program advertising Houdini's open challenge to mediums, circa 1924.

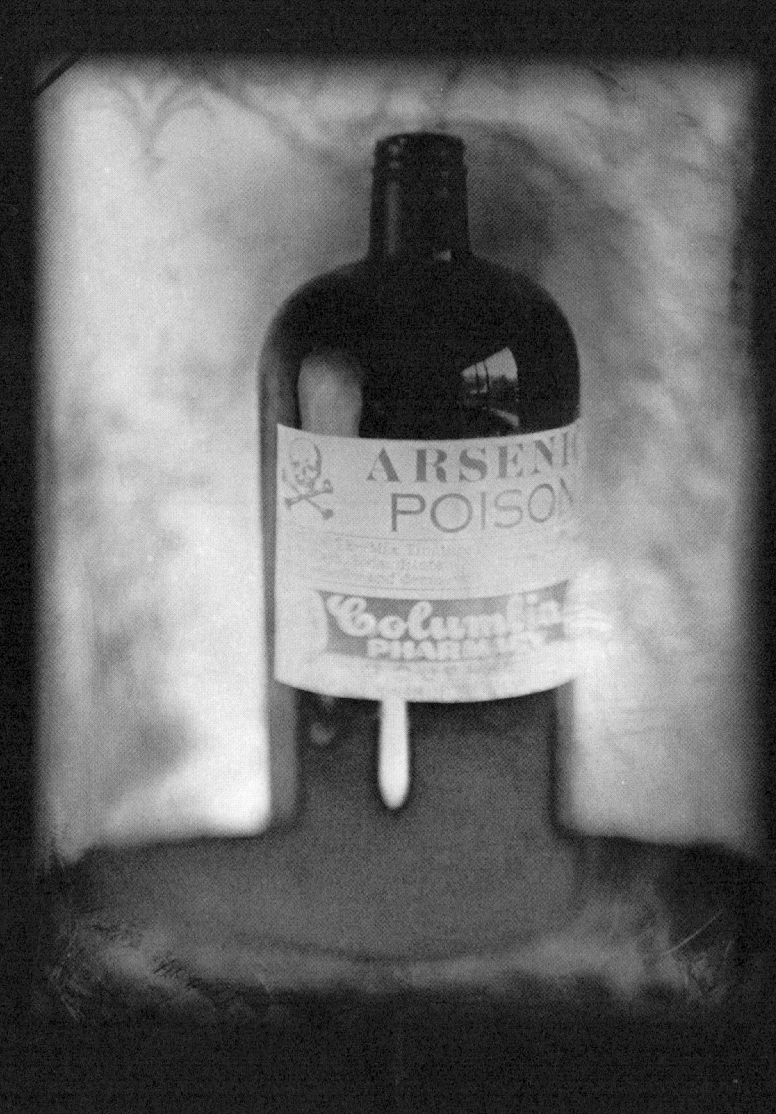

SEVEN

A Menace to Health
and Sanity

*"How long a private friendship can survive
such an ordeal I do not know, but at least
I did not create the situation."*
~ Sir Arthur Conan Doyle

T he fragile peace between Houdini and Doyle depended on Houdini's silence, his willingness to tread softly around the topic of Spiritualism. But it wasn't his nature to sit things out. Inside, he was seething. He didn't like feeling misrepresented or the sensation of being a pawn in his friend's evangelical campaign. Houdini respected and admired Doyle for his mind and his worldly success. He may even have been intimidated by a fame greater than his own, one rooted in intellectual achievement and social status rather than strength, skill, and spectacle.

When he finally expressed his views on Spiritualism, Houdini did so for the world to hear, in an article in the *New York Sun* titled "Spirit Compacts Unfilled."

All of his many investigations, he wrote, had left him unconvinced about the "possibility of communication with the loved ones who have gone beyond."

His article winged its way across the Atlantic to Sir Arthur, who was stunned. What about Atlantic City? the writer fired back in a letter. "I saw what you got and what the effect was upon you at the time."

Doyle resisted what must have been a fierce urge to publish a rebuttal: "I have no fancy for sparring with a friend in public." But they had reached an impasse. "I have done my best to give you the truth," Doyle said. "There are lots of other subjects on which we can all meet in friendly converse."

For a while longer, the friends agreed to disagree, but Houdini liked being censored even less than he liked being quiet; he responded to Doyle's disapproval with sarcasm: "You write that you are very sore. I trust it is not with me, because you, having been truthful and manly all your life, naturally must admire the same traits in other human beings."

He let on, at last, that the Atlantic City séance had been, for him, a bust, though he hadn't said so at the time. He had wanted so much to hear from his mother that he hushed his doubts about the crosses marked on Lady Doyle's pages and Cecilia Weiss's sudden and inexplicable mastery of the English language.

Doyle struck back in a letter:

> I read an interview you gave some American paper the other day, in which you said my wife gave you nothing striking when she wrote for you. When you met us, three days after the writing, in New York, you said—"I have been walking on air ever since," or words to that effect. I wonder how you reconcile your various utterances!

After a bit of private sparring, their argument migrated into the *New York Times* when Houdini bragged in an interview that he could re-create any medium's feats using just the tools of the magician's trade. The paper credited him as having attended, by way of research, ten thousand séances. Doyle wrote in to scoff. To attend that many sittings, Houdini would need to visit a medium every day for thirty years! Doyle was personally aware of Houdini visiting only two mediums: Eva C. and Mrs. Wriedt. And how could he presume to reunite Sir Arthur with his mother and son—as Doyle believed, *knew* a medium had done—using *magic tricks*?

A few weeks later, Houdini was back for another round in the *Times*; he pointed out that many of the mediums who had restored Doyle to his family beyond the veil had since been called out or even arrested for fraud.

Again, Doyle refrained from public debate, but acknowledged, "Our relations are certainly curious and likely to become more so, for as long as you attack what *I know* from experience to be true I have no alternative but to attack you in turn."

Doyle would soon be back in New York on his second North American tour to promote Spiritualism. The papers were eager to nudge the two celebrities back into the ring, in order to increase their own circulation numbers. The *New York Mail* thundered, "Sir Arthur Coming to Answer Houdini," but as it turned out, when the Doyles arrived, Houdini was out west touring.

Perhaps to draw a clean line between his Spiritualism—a religious worldview with its own theology and philosophy—and the parlor tricks of false spirit mediums who often learned their methods from magicians, Doyle ridiculed the latter in print: magicians were "harmless and ingenious amusers of society" who took on "airs of superior intelligence."

He received, in turn, a winking invitation to attend the Society of American Magicians (SAM) Carnival of Magic benefit in New York. The magicians promised to whip up spirit photographs and wax spirit hands for the occasion.

This kind of distinction between true and false Spiritualism would certainly have stirred up Houdini's insecurities about his intellectual status in relation to Doyle—and put added stress on a friendship already hanging by a thread.

It seems no coincidence that while Doyle's tour bristled with controversy, Houdini was engineering a new job description. By February 1924, he had signed on for a lecture tour of his own, twenty-four stops, mainly in the South and Midwest. He would turn fifty years old in April, and though this wasn't exactly retirement, *Billboard* announced, "Houdini, the magician, has become Houdini, the educator!" Here was his chance to rival the likes of Sir Arthur and other "intelligentsa [*sic*]."

Houdini's handwritten list of original slides used for his lectures on Spiritualism, circa 1922.

"Wait till Sir A. C. Doyle hears of my lectures!" he wrote in his diary. Like any Houdini performance, his down-to-earth, hands-on presentations—with fifty colored slides illustrating a lively history of Spiritualism—gripped audiences. Houdini not only told his crowds how fakes made spirit hands or conjured messages on slates, he showed them, often step-by-step.

His tour was extended for two months by popular demand, and more and more often, journalists, religious groups, and radio stations called on Houdini as an expert. Soon, many viewed him as *the* expert on matters mysterious and "psychical."

Children attend Houdini's exposé of fraudulent mediums, circa 1925.

He pooled the rich material he had compiled for the lectures into *A Magician Among the Spirits*, what would be his best-known book, published in the late spring of 1924.

He devoted a chapter and several detours to his friend (though little now remained of that friendship) Sir Arthur Conan Doyle. He wanted "no warfare" with Sir Arthur and had no wish to discredit him,

☞ Houdini Lends a Hand

When Sir Arthur visited his home early in their friendship, Houdini explained how easy it was to make "spirit hands." The props turned up often at séances, eerie and luminous, floating in the dark (strung from fishing line manipulated by a medium or confederate). The disembodied hands might even reach out and touch, with clammy tenderness, the face or hair of a séance sitter. To make them, Houdini later demonstrated, all you had to do was blow up a rubber glove and dip the glove in paraffin wax. When the wax cooled, you deflated and removed the glove, leaving a shapely hand behind.

Houdini making spirit hands, circa 1923.

but more and more Houdini believed it was his duty to seek and tell the truth, and that truth wasn't pretty.

An alarming side effect of Doyle's US talks the year before had been a rash of suicides and murders by deranged people who had taken his descriptions of a beautiful afterlife literally. News sources may have exaggerated the numbers (or skewed the context), but a few cases seemed sensational proof of Houdini's claims that the "craze" or "cult" of Spiritualism had become "a menace to health and sanity."

A testimonial from warden James Harris describing Houdini's dramatic escape from "Murderers' Row."

JAMES H. HARRIS, WARDEN

W. GRAYSON URNER, DEPUTY WARDEN.

United States Jail,

Washington, D. C., January 6th, 1906

This is to certify that Mr. Harry Houdini, at the United States Jail today, was stripped stark naked, thoroughly searched, and locked up in cell No. 2 of the South Wing,--the cell in which Charles J. Guiteau, the assassinator of President Garfield, was confined during his incarceration, from the date of his commitment, July 2nd, 1881, until the day on which he was executed, June 30th, 1882. Mr. Houdini, in about two minutes, managed to escape from that cell, and then broke into the cell in which his clothing was locked up. He then proceeded to release from their cells all the prisoners on the ground floor. There was positively no chance for any confederacy or collusion.

Mr. Houdini accomplished all of the above-mentioned facts, in addition to putting on all his clothing, in twenty-one minutes.

J H Harris

Warden United States Jail, D. C.

☞ Houdini Escapes from Assassin's Cell!

Early in his escape career, on January 6, 1906, Houdini had pulled off a much-publicized escape from the Washington, DC, jail cell that had once held Charles J. Guiteau, the assassin of President Garfield. It's interesting that Guiteau was, according to Houdini, an early "victim" of the madness he claimed was spawned by the "cult" of Spiritualism. Guiteau, a Spiritualist, claimed spirits told him to kill the president.

Houdini tells of a young Barnard College student, Miss Marie Bloomfield, "who declared herself in love with a Spirit and finally was driven to suicide in order to join him."

On April 15, three days after Doyle's first Carnegie Hall lecture, a *New York Times* headline read: "Wife Seeks Death to Be a Spirit Guide: Newark Woman Kills Baby, Then Drinks Poison So She May Help Husband from Beyond." The woman's husband blamed the deaths on his wife's ill health and interest in Spiritualism; he published her suicide note in accordance with her wishes. The paper followed up with Doyle, who said, "The incident shows the great danger of the present want of knowledge concerning spiritual matters." Two days later, the *Times* ran a story about a man in San Francisco who had, according to police, shot and killed two of his boys, ages seven and eight. The man, John Cornyn, claimed to be in "communication" with his dead wife, who had "asked him to send all of their five children to her."

"It is with the deepest interest and concern," Houdini wrote, "that I have watched this great wave of Spiritualism sweep the world in recent months and realized that it has taken such a hold on persons of a neurotic temperament, especially those suffering from bereavement."

To Doyle, these tragedies were a grave misunderstanding of the message of Spiritualism. "Truth wins and there is lots of time."

"**The first thing** *the knowledge of Spiritualism does for you is to remove all fear of death. A Spiritualist fears death no more than walking into the next room— it is a promotion to a life far more lovely and happy than the earth-life.*" —LADY DOYLE, FROM A RADIO SPEECH IN NEW YORK, 1923

Houdini argues in *A Magician Among the Spirits* that even medical professionals expressed concern about the effects of Spiritualism on fragile minds. In an annual report in 1920, an eminent physician and asylum superintendent acknowledged that many people had "broken down since the war" and had taken up Spiritualism as "a solace to their feelings." Another doctor predicted that "asylums would be flooded if popular taste did not swing to more wholesome diversions." A third estimated some million cases of insanity under the influence of Spiritualism.

When Houdini called attention to these numbers, Doyle argued in his jovial way, "People have been going mad for years, and you will find on investigation that many go mad on other subjects besides Spiritualism."

The average person didn't "realize the suffering, losses, misfortunes, crimes and atrocities" that were a direct result of the

☞ Fingerprinting a Spirit

One of the most "startling swindles" Houdini recalls in *A Magician Among the Spirits* originated with a sculptor "who dabbled some in Spiritualism." The man managed to make a plaster of paris mold of a dead man's fingertips and filled it with a rubbery substance that, when hardened, matched the corpse's fingers exactly. The cunning medium planted a few prints on a trumpet for that night's séance. Discussion led to an investigation, and sure enough, the dead fellow in the morgue looked to have left his prints on the horn.

Another medium got hold of this trick and secured a job in a funeral home, where he eventually collected the prints of a number of well-heeled dead. "There are two cases on record," Houdini writes, "where fortunes were at stake because of this sort of fraud."

"curse" of Spiritualism, Houdini believed, and his intention was to right that.

For long stretches, *A Magician Among the Spirits* reads like a rap sheet of the movement's seedy underside, with Houdini listing key players and colorfully narrating the grifts and grafts committed in its name, everything from jewelry theft and bum real-estate deals (on the advice of "spirits") to corpses used for purposes of fraud. Widows were cheated out of hefty fortunes and husbands out of peace of mind:

> *The* **Washington Times** *(D.C.) of January 14, 1923, tells of an Earl L. Clark who secured a divorce on the grounds that his wife claimed that she had a "Spirit Affinity" named Alfred and that this Alfred through Clark's wife made his life unbearable, even predicting his death so that she might marry some man who would "accept Alfred's Spiritual guidance."*

In most of these cases, Houdini observed, people didn't suspect the medium in the least: "The majority of people who are fleeced . . . really believe that the Spirit of their departed one prescribed the loss." It was only when mediums fell out with each other, when "honor among thieves" broke down, that fraud came to the attention of the police.

Two mediums he notes as especially skilled at fraud and deception were his contemporary Ann O'Delia Diss Debar (a master criminal who practiced hypnosis and mediumship as handy sidelines) and the legendary physical medium Daniel Dunglas (D. D.) Home.

Houdini calls both "adventurers" with a knack for infiltrating high society, "bringing within their reach people of wealth as well as scholars and scientists." He claimed that all other

The medium Ann O'Delia Diss Debar, 1909.

mediums combined "could not have aggregated the amount of money obtained by these two."

Debar was an outright fraud (he includes her arrest record as an appendix in his book), "one of the most extraordinary fake mediums and mystery swindlers the world has ever known. Some even classed her among the ten most prominent and dangerous female criminals of the world." Debar changed locales as often as she did her name, claiming at one point to be "the daughter of King Louis I of Bavaria and Lola Montez, a Spanish-Irish dancer." Her schemes were elaborate and ambitious, targeting aristocratic "marks" and magnates of Wall Street. "It was not unusual," he wrote, "for her to make deals that ran into the hundreds of thousands of dollars."

Of the multitude of mediums who rose up in the shadow of the Fox sisters, Houdini counted fewer than a dozen "whose work, in spite of repeated exposure, is still pointed to as proof of Spiritualism." Chief among them was

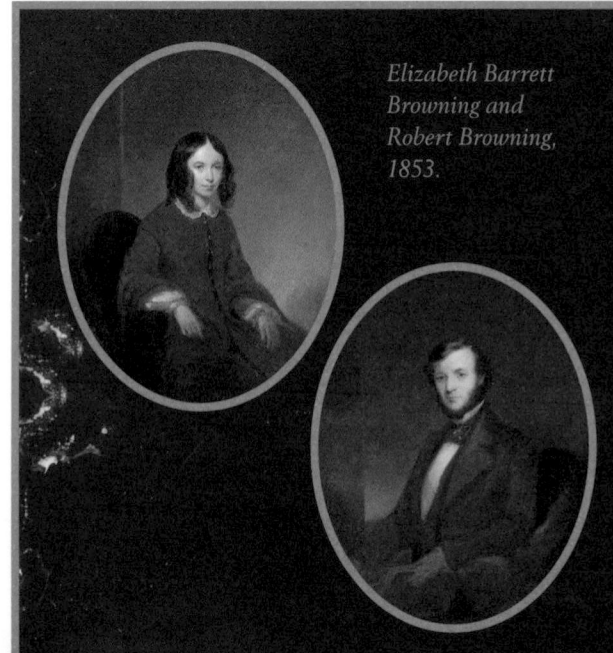

Elizabeth Barrett Browning and Robert Browning, 1853.

the Scottish medium D. D. Home, who peaked between 1859 and 1872.

Magnetic and cultured, musical and artistic, elegant and educated in both medicine and linguistics, Home was a snappy dresser and fond of diamonds, rubies, and other fine jewelry. Tuberculosis gave him a pale, ethereal quality that together with silvery eyes and copper hair made him look otherworldly. He inspired trust, awe, and sympathy, and built his success and reputation by *not* charging money for his services as a medium (a clever maneuver that protected him from skeptics: as a fellow visitor in the house, an unpaid member of the host's inner circle, he was unlikely to be challenged or called out during a séance, the rudeness of which would insult the host).

Undated portrait of the Scottish medium D. D. Home.

🖝 How Do I Distrust Thee? Let Me Count the Ways

The famous poet Elizabeth Barrett Browning was enchanted by D. D. Home and wholly convinced, but her equally esteemed husband, Robert Browning, was no fan. After his adored wife's death, he published a scathing poem based on Home.

"Now, don't, sir! Don't expose me!
Just this once!
This was the first and only time, I'll
swear,—

Look at me,—see, I kneel,—the
only time,
I swear, I ever cheated,—yes, by
the soul
Of Her who hears—(your sainted
mother, sir!)
All except this last accident, was
truth—"

—ROBERT BROWNING,
FROM "MR. SLUDGE, 'THE MEDIUM'"

The poet Elizabeth Barrett Browning wrote, after a sitting with Home, "We were touched by the invisible." And in fact, Home's séances were a dazzling spectacle: objects bobbed around the room on air, ghostly hands reached out to touch sitters, firefly lights glinted and faded. Knocks raced over walls, barely audible voices whispered in corners, the *swish* of wings filled the dark.

Home lived "a life of positive luxury" in America and Europe on the hospitality of Spiritualist friends who competed to host him at their estates for extended periods and wooed him with gifts (gifts often "suggested" by the spirits: "His spirit guide seems to have always kept a sharp eye on his need for earthly sustenance," said Houdini).

Born in Scotland in 1833, Home came to New York from Edinburgh as a child and lived with his pious aunt. When he informed her of his plans to be a medium, she called him a devil and threw a chair at him. And so, says Houdini, began Home's "custom of living on the bounty of friends and dupes."

Home's clients and friends were usually people of culture, rank, and wealth—even royalty, including the emperor and empress of France and the czar of Russia. Like the occult "healer" Rasputin, Home lived at court in the Russian palace for weeks at a time. He twice married Russian noblewomen, and before he left Russia, he made some emeralds conveniently "dematerialize" at court (the police made the jewels "rematerialize" and invited him to leave the country).

In England in 1859, Home charmed Mrs. Lyons, a seventy-five-year-old widow, and burned her will. She signed over money and real estate before panicking and filing a suit to retrieve the sixty thousand pounds he had relieved her of. In his closing remarks, a court official called the widow's mind "saturated with delusion." As for Spiritualism, he said, it was on the evidence a "system of mischievous nonsense well calculated to delude the vain, the weak, the foolish, and the superstitious."

"The average medium works only for the money he or she can extract from the public," Houdini concluded, reviewing the crimes and consequences of spirit fraud, "money obtained by moving the deepest sentiments in the human soul." Spiritualism was "nothing more or less than mental intoxication," as bad as alcohol or drugs. Why, he wondered, were those vices legally prohibited (both were, in the 1920s, in the United States) when fake mediums had license to drain "every bit of reason and common sense from their victims. . . . It ought to be stopped," he told his readers, "it must be stopped."

An illustration of the medium D. D. Home apparently levitating himself in front of witnesses on August 8, 1852.

🖝 Out One Window, In the Other

The physical medium D. D. Home was best known for his dramatic levitation acts and for a feat Houdini called his "masterpiece": sailing out a window feetfirst, floating another seven or more feet away, and landing catlike in the room across the alley, where he calmly strode to a chair and sat down. Then, to the startled cries of his group, he did it again, passing back—stiffly horizontal, they reported—through the original window again. Or so the story goes. Houdini offered a do-over of Home's famous feat "under the same conditions," but Spiritualists never took up his challenge. "I desire to go on record as being able to perform the same phenomena," he insists in *A Magician Among the Spirits.* The "mind of the average person accepts what it sees," he complains, "and is not willing to apply the laws of physics."

PART THREE

Not a Skeptic

EIGHT

Science and Sincerity

*"Psychical science, as we here try to pursue
it, is the embryo of something which in time
may dominate the whole world of thought."*

~*Sir William Crookes,*
IN AN 1897 SPR PRESIDENTIAL ADDRESS

"Gladly would I embrace Spiritualism if it could prove its claims," Houdini liked to say, and from the first, intelligent people tried. Both sincere believers like Sir Arthur Conan Doyle and doubters like Houdini used scientific methods to observe, classify, and, as needs be, rule out spiritual phenomena.

Houdini applauded these efforts and joined in when he could. Like many magicians, he saw himself at the far side of a continuum, with fraud and superstition on the one end and entertainment and delight in the marvelous on the other.

But scientists, he argued, were as likely to be duped as anyone, and for the same reasons. In an aside in his book *Miracle Mongers and Their Methods*, Houdini classifies scientists as either "serious-minded"—hard at work solving natural mysteries and benefiting humankind—or "credulous" and "wonder-loving."

Science failed, he argued, when investigators were blind to "the flimsy juggling of pseudo-mediums."

Houdini maintained that the wonder-loving scientist was easy to lead and easy to fool. Many of these great minds were, like his friend Sir Arthur, "fortified in their belief by grief." The number one barrier to their success as investigators was their "perfect willingness to be deceived," an eagerness that actually helped mediums produce fraudulent results.

It was no accident, Houdini believed, that brilliant, rational men like Sir Arthur and Sir Oliver Lodge—a renowned physicist and psychic researcher who eventually converted to Spiritualism—embraced the faith after losing sons in the war.

To Houdini's mind, these were grieving men determined to see what they wanted to see, evidence or no evidence. Doyle had all but said so: "The objective side of it ceased to interest, for having made up one's mind that it was true there was an end of the matter." When Houdini called him on this statement, Doyle claimed that his investment in Spiritualism began two years *before* his son Kingsley's death, in a mood of universal inquiry.

As for Sir Oliver Lodge, Houdini saw no other explanation for why one of England's most honored scientists would "permit his pen to lay before a thinking world" impossibilities like this:

> *A table can exhibit hesitation, it can seek for information, it can welcome a newcomer, it can indicate joy or sorrow, fun or gravity, it can keep time with a song as if joining in the chorus and most notably of all it can exhibit affection in an unmistakable manner.*

"*What has all this to do with the spirit of the departed?*" Houdini ranted.

How is it possible to accept such silly nonsense? Think of it! A table *with intelligence, brains—a* table *with consciousness—a* table *with emotion. Yet that is the sort of reasoning used by Sir Oliver in his book, "Raymond." . . . When we read of a mind of such high culture being overcome by such misfortune we are moved to compassion.*

Sir Oliver's grief following the death of his son, Raymond, in the war made him, in other words, an easy mark, just like Sir Arthur.

DURING DOYLE'S SECOND AMERICAN TOUR AND Houdini's western excursion in 1923, both men and their families wound up registered at the Brown Palace Hotel in Denver.

A local paper got wind of it and published a sensational headline: "DOYLE IN DENVER DEFIES HOUDINI."

Doyle had, the reporter claimed, challenged Houdini to honor his boast and re-create séance phenomena using only a magician's tricks. The manifestation Doyle had in mind? Houdini must reunite Doyle with "the Ma'am," Doyle's mother, at a wager of five thousand dollars.

Doyle scoffed at the headline. He would never propose such a "blasphemous and absurd" thing, and Houdini—used to being misquoted and misrepresented in print—believed him. But their recent sharp exchanges in the New York press had wrecked their mutual trust.

Though they met several times in Denver, even visiting a local spirit photographer together, their friendship was now strained to the point of snapping. They couldn't get past their arguments—the Atlantic City séance, Eva C., William Hope and the Crewe Circle— or ignore incompatible worldviews and a swelling resentment.

"There is nothing that Sir Arthur will believe that surprises me," Houdini complained.

Doyle admitted that he found Houdini's prejudice, vanity, and fixation on publicity distasteful.

And after another squabble, over a manuscript that Houdini believed Doyle had promised him, they parted ways.

"I am very sorry this breach has come," said Sir Arthur, "but 'friendly is as friendly does,' and this is not friendly." He returned to England, and despite one more exchange of letters—and a continued professional interest in each other—the two men never met again.

SPIRITUALISM (AND IN MANY WAYS, SIR ARTHUR) had helped Houdini earn the intellectual credibility he had always wanted. These days he was corresponding with the inventor Thomas Edison and playing golf with poet and writer Carl Sandburg. He was more than a respected entertainer; he was important, someone his rabbi father would have been proud of.

Houdini's lecture tour and book were his ticket to continued success at a time when his physical strength and dexterity were winding down. He also just enjoyed showing up Sir Arthur, outing clever (but not clever enough) mediums, and grading and participating in scientific investigations.

By Houdini's day, there had already been a number of notable attempts by science to wade into the murky waters of psychic investigation.

In the early 1870s, English chemist and physicist Sir William Crookes—who served as president of the SPR for several years and later of a like organization called the Ghost Club—observed some of the most celebrated mediums of his day, including Kate Fox and D. D. Home.

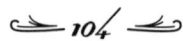

"There is not the slightest doubt in my mind that this brainy man was hoodwinked," Houdini believed. Even if investigators were not—like Doyle and Lodge—in a crisis of grief, they were susceptible, under close quarters and in the forced intimacy of the séance room, to a range of other emotions.

Other critics of Crookes agreed, attributing his tendency to rule in favor of fraudulent mediums to gullibility, poor eyesight, and, in the case of a fetching young medium named Florence Cook, romantic involvement.

Crookes perfectly illustrated Houdini's argument that scientists were only human, inexperienced with bald (and often artful) deception, and easily duped. They certainly weren't "immune from the influence of *personal magnetism*," of which mediums

The ghostly "materialization" of Katie King (who much resembled the attending medium, Florence Cook) on the arm of physicist Sir William Crookes, 1874.

like Cook and Home had plenty. Though his psychic research was discredited, Sir William Crookes was one of the first modern scientists to allow for the existence of paranormal forces that science could not (yet) explain.

The Seybert Commission, formed at the University of Pennsylvania from a bequest by Spiritualist Henry Seybert—Houdini could think of no "fairer-minded and more impartial" committee—met in the 1880s to assess slate-writing medium Henry Slade and others. Their report opens with a nod to Spiritualism as a religion. The members of the group were "deeply impressed with the seriousness of their undertaking" and felt all compassion for "crushed and bleeding hearts" in search of hope and consolation. Nothing in their report, they urged, should be seen as "indicating indifference or levity."

But the tone of the report is usually exasperated. Like Houdini, the committee grumped about the requirement of darkness and other unscientific conditions mediums imposed: "No one . . . can demand of us that we should accept profound mysteries with our eyes tight shut, and our hands fast closed, and with every avenue to our reasoning faculties insurmountably barred."

Overall, the committee found "an unwillingness on the part of Mediums to have their powers freely and thoroughly investigated"—a fact that made the work "difficult and expensive."

Despite rules that made it hard to judge with clear eyes, the Seybert Commission ruled Slade's work fraudulent without a doubt: "This phenomenon can be performed by legerdemain [sleight of hand]."

In addition to slate writing, the Seybert Commission investigated spirit rapping and other manifestations. Their report, published in 1887, left no room for doubt: "We have not been cheered in our investigations by the discovery of a single novel fact." Spiritualist phenomena were not only sheer fraud inflicted on an unsuspecting public, they were also tedious.

The report may have convinced some but did little to stem the flow of inquiry. In a materialist age where the boundaries of faith and science were on everyone's mind—and the question of life after death on everyone's lips—unorthodox scientists were venturing into all branches of paranormal study, from clairvoyance to poltergeists. A doctor in Haverhill, Massachusetts, attempted to weigh the soul (according to his calculations, a body lost—give or take—twenty-one grams when a spirit vacated at death). Even Charles Darwin's colleague and collaborator Alfred Russel Wallace wondered about those mysteries which "science ignored because it could not explain."

One line of investigation that Houdini may not have been aware of—or chose not to feature in his exposé—was a study by the American branch of the Society for Psychical Research (ASPR) of the trance medium Leonora Piper.

In the beginning, the ASPR was a small band of curious (and courageous; their quest to explore the likes of ESP and survival after death was soundly ridiculed by mainstream science) re-searchers headed by psychologist William James.

Though the debate of the day was lively, the mysteries posed by Spiritualism were not new. Look back, James pointed out, and "you will find there was never a time when these things were not reported just as abundantly as they are today. . . . The phenomena are there, lying broadcast over the surface of history."

The investigation into Leonora Piper gripped James and his ASPR colleagues perhaps more than any other, leading to more than two decades of research.

When she was eight years old in Nashua, New Hampshire, circa 1865, Leonora was playing in the garden when something slammed into her right ear. She heard a hissing. The *hiss* became an "s" and then a name—"Sara"—and the name stretched into a sentence. Leonora ran indoors howling for her mother and ex-plained, through sobs: "Something hit me on the ear and Aunt Sara said she wasn't dead but with you still!"

The girl's alarm alarmed her mother, who scribbled down what had happened.

Less than a week later, a letter arrived. Her aunt had died on the same day, around the time of the incident in the garden.

Leonora's family wanted nothing to do with spirit phenomena and worked hard to move past it. They would have known about children like the Fox sisters, who were paraded about as spectacles. It was no life for a child from a respectable, churchgoing family. They did their best to ignore the event and all it suggested.

Years later, after she married and moved to Boston, Leonora visited a healer who billed himself as clairvoyant, for help with an old injury that doctors seemed unable to diagnose or soothe. The moment the psychic touched her, her head swarmed with voices and she fell down, entering her own trance; so began a reluctant career as a psychic medium.

Word circulated fast, and strangers began to show up at her door on Beacon Hill. One of them, in the late summer of 1885, was the widowed Eliza Gibbens, mother-in-law of the ASPR's William James, who was astonished and told her eminent son-in-law so.

James scheduled his own visit with Mrs. Piper. He was surprised, at his sitting, to find none of the usual props: bells and trumpets, chairs in a circle, mahogany cabinets. Just a plain, soft-spoken woman in a chair, who apologized that there would be no sensational spirit shows in her parlor; there might, in fact, be nothing at all. She would enter a trance and see what her spirit guide had in mind.

William James, who came in skeptical, left convinced. He enlisted twenty-five associates to book sittings with Mrs. Piper, so they might compare notes—the beginnings of an investigation that would last, off and on, until Piper retired in 1927.

In his 1896 ASPR presidential address, James argued that a single instance could undermine any "universal proposition." It might be true that most mediums were frauds, deceiving the innocent and gullible; but what if one, just one, were genuine? It was a game changer, he argued, or could be:

If you wish to upset the law that all crows are black, you mustn't seek to show that no crows are; it is enough if you prove one single crow to be white. My own white crow is Mrs. Piper. In the trances of this medium, I cannot resist the conviction that knowledge appears which she has never gained by the ordinary waking use of her eyes and ears and wits.

Had Houdini investigated Piper, would she have swayed him? The clear advantage of being a mental over a physical medium is that there are no revealing clues—doll heads, regurgitated fabric, phosphorous oil—to expose. There's no hard evidence. Investigators can only trace the medium's data to an "earthly" source or catch her or him in the furtive act of gathering intelligence. A frustrating position for a skeptic—something Houdini repeatedly denied he was.

"I am not a scoffer," he argued. "I firmly believe in a Supreme Being and that there is a Hereafter." In fact, the first stop he made whenever he returned from a trip was to the "hallowed spot" where his beloved parents were buried. "Both promised me faithfully innumerable times in this life that if they could aid and protect me from their graves or from the Great Beyond, they would do so. My mind has always been open and receptive and ready to believe. . . . I am not a skeptic. . . . If convincing evidence is brought forward I will be the first to acknowledge my mistake."

NINE

It Takes a Flimflammer
to Catch a Flimflammer

*"All mediums hate to have a magician attend
a séance."*
                                   ~Harry Houdini

The Seybert Commission's ruling against the slate writer Henry Slade had been partly a commonsense call. The writing on Slade's slates fell into two classes: writing that answered specific, real-time questions and writing that came as voluntary "contributions" from spirits. The replies (dashed off in the heat of the moment) were a "crude scrawl, abrupt in composition, and often almost or quite illegible." The others were neat and tidy, careful "even to punctuation"; investigators concluded that these contributed slates were carefully prepared in advance and slipped into the proceedings.

But the real exposure began when Seybert investigators, in the spirit of a magician's debunking, introduced sleight of hand of their own: "One of our number, on three occasions, [used] a pocket mirror, carefully adjusted" to watch what was happening under the table. Unknown to Slade, the mirror "gave back the reflection of fingers, which were clearly not Spiritual, opening the slates and writing the answer."

In *A Magician Among the Spirits*, Houdini cheers this approach: "The only way to conduct a successful [investigation] is to get the committee together previous to the séance, discuss the expected manifestations, formulate some plan for concerted action and if possible assign each member some specific part." What's more, he said, "These parts should be rehearsed." (Spoken like a true showman.)

The commission not only refused to sit passively by in the dark while their subjects staged deception, they later invited "an eminent professional juggler" and friend of Houdini's, master magician Harry Kellar, to demonstrate his own slate writing methods, but without pretense of assistance from Beyond.

Houdini with magician Harry Kellar, circa 1912.

Throughout the 1880s, Kellar had demonstrated methods for table tipping, spirit materialization, and other phenomena at his own shows. For the commission, the magician performed "independent slate-writing far more remarkable" than any medium's. They were baffled.

Kellar had done the deed in broad daylight, first presenting a slate, perfectly clean on both sides. He held the slate and a stub of slate pencil under the leaf of the table the group was seated around. "Our eyes never for a fraction of a second lost sight of [the magician's] thumb," the 1887 report claimed. "It never moved; and yet in a few minutes the slate was produced, covered on both sides with writing."

Kellar had far outperformed Slade, producing messages not only in English but in Chinese, Dutch, French, Japanese, Spanish, and Gujerati. His method? He'd paid the hotel owner to let him construct a trapdoor in the floor of the room, and then laid a cushy rug over it. His assistant, Barney, had stood at attention below the floor with a variety of slates.

"A fake, pure and simple," Kellar remarked. "But that's what all Spiritualistic manifestations are."

☞ On to Safer Swindles

"Spirit slates," Houdini wrote in 1924, "are now listed in the catalogues of houses dealing in conjuring apparatus and the fraud mediums who formerly made use of them are employing the safer and easier swindles of automatic writing, trance or trumpet messages, and the 'ouija board.'"

Slate with a chalk message ostensibly from the spirit of Abraham Lincoln via the medium Pierre L. O. A. Keeler (date unknown).

The courts also made use of magicians' expertise to reveal fraud. P. T. Barnum (who had guest-starred at the trial of spirit photographer William Mumler) wasn't the only showman officially summoned to expose "humbug." In 1888, popular magician Alexander Herrmann gave a public demonstration at Manhattan's Academy of Music. To help aid investigators and inform the public, he duplicated table tipping, spirit materialization, and other tricks used by the medium Ann O'Delia Diss Debar to swindle her victims.

In the heyday of both magic and Spiritualism, fake spirit mediums were often magicians gone rogue. "It is much more lucrative to be a charlatan medium," Houdini observed, "than an honest magician." Fellow illusionists knew better how to set traps and prove trickery than "the grave scientist" who set out to "solve the problem by mathematics or logic."

Sir Arthur spoke of seeing spirit manifestations "with my own eyes" or hearing spirit voices "with my own ears," and to Houdini's mind, sight and hearing were the weakest and most easily deceived of the senses.

☞ Why Did They Do It?

Though he questioned her authenticity and intent (as he did the motives of most mediums), Houdini credits Eusapia Palladino "in her crafty prime" as a master of misdirection. Born into extreme poverty in the Neapolitan district of Italy and orphaned as a child, Palladino was uneducated and largely illiterate, but managed to bamboozle "more philosophic and scientific men than any other known medium." Houdini, who as a boy of twelve had run away from home to escape the indignities of poverty, reveals a grudging respect for Palladino's origin story. Taken in by an "acrobat or conjurer" at thirteen, she learned quickly—and found her ticket out—as a "professional phenomena producer."

As the response of Leonora Piper's family to her gift shows, this line of work wasn't a respectable employment avenue in the nineteenth and early twentieth

Like magicians, mediums were experts at calculated misdirection, shifting clients' attention away from one (suspect) behavior with another brighter, bigger, or louder one. Houdini had it "on good authority," for example, that the famous Italian medium Eusapia Palladino "threw her legs into the laps of her male sitters . . . placed her head upon their shoulders, and did various other things calculated to confuse and muddle men, all of which was explained on the theory of 'hysteria.'" It was no wonder, he argued, that "a lot of old scientists were badly flabbergasted by such conduct."

Misdirection by mediums led to "mal-observation" by scientists—what Houdini calls "the curse of investigation," giving mediums the "power to divert the attention, carrying it at will to any place they wish and numbing the subconscious mind."

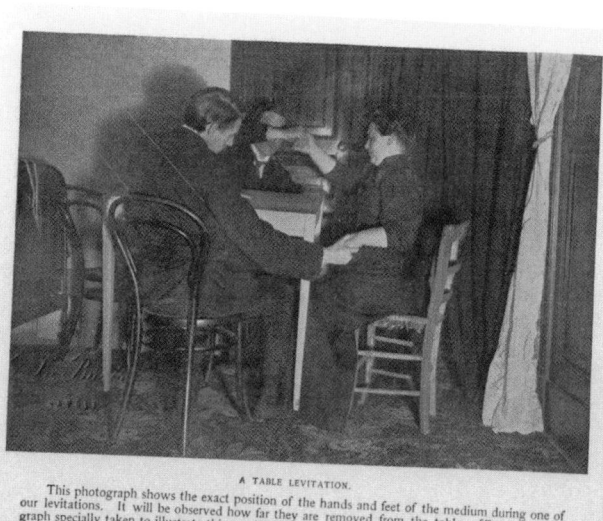

The medium Eusapia Palladino levitates a table during a séance, 1909.

A TABLE LEVITATION.

This photograph shows the exact position of the hands and feet of the medium during one of our levitations. It will be observed how far they are removed from the table. [From a photograph specially taken to illustrate this manifestation.]

centuries. (Though it might invite wealth and even fame, it might also lead to despair, drink, and dissolution, as it had for the Fox sisters.) But for underprivileged women like Palladino and the sisters, an exotic career as a spirit medium may have beat out their other options. It was a novel way to make a living at a time when poor women had very few avenues open to them, other than marriage or domestic service.

It didn't help that the people who attended séances were most often a willing audience. They came with hope, longing to hear from the other side. "This love of the dead really is at the bottom of the present experiments," Houdini told the *New York Times* in an interview exposing the tricks of the medium trade. Even if a sitter wasn't waiting on the edge of her or his seat in the dark to hear from a lost friend or relative, *all* human beings suffered similar hardships: broken hearts, empty pockets, fear. Most people were not only willing but eager to be rewarded with manifesta-

☞ Supplying Peculiar Effects

Like Houdini, magician William Marriott exposed fake mediums. He also brought to the public eye a rare catalog titled *Gambols with the Ghosts: Mind Reading, Spiritualistic Effects, Mental and Psychical Phenomena and Horoscopy*, published in 1901 by Ralph E. Sylvestre of Chicago. Offering tools for fake slate writing, self-playing guitars, self-rapping tables, materializations, and a "Complete Spiritualistic Séance," the catalog circulated quietly with the understanding that it would be returned to Sylvestre together with orders. "Our experience during the past thirty years in supplying mediums and others with the peculiar effects," stated its introduction, "enable us to place before you only those which are practical and of use. . . . We wish you to thoroughly appreciate that, while we do not, for obvious reasons, mention the names of our clients and their work (they being kept in strict confidence, the same as a physician treats his patients), we can furnish you with the explanation and, where necessary, the materials for the production of any known public 'tests' or 'phenomena' not mentioned in this, our latest list. You are aware that our effects are being used by nearly all prominent mediums . . . of the entire world." Marriott purchased some of these illusions and posed for photographs.

(Left) The cover of Ralph E. Sylvestre's Gambols with the Ghosts *catalog, 1901. (Right) Magician William Marriott posing with "ghosts" ordered from the catalog, 1910.*

tions and soft words; they were open to suggestion. "One little sign even," said Houdini, "appeals to their waiting imagination, shatters all ordinary caution and they are converted."

Skilled mediums could lull clients into a kind of self-hypnosis or, by reading facial cues, sense when their guesses were getting warmer. But it was because the mediums were tuned in to the sitters, Houdini said, *not* to the departed.

As for hands and accordions flying around in the dark, it was not "unusual for the eye or ear to play tricks."

Houdini admitted that even he had been "deceived once or twice by a new illusion, but if my mind, which has been so keenly trained for years to invent mysterious effects, can be deceived, how much more susceptible must the ordinary observer be."

Even the infamous Davenport brothers were foiled in the end by another magician—or an aspiring one. English stage magician and inventor John Nevil Maskelyne, the first in a succession of Maskelyne magicians, exposed the brothers after figuring out their technique at an 1865 show. Beams of sunlight filtering between closed drapes had exposed a crack in the famous Davenport cabinet, and through it, Maskelyne glimpsed a hand ringing a bell. Eureka! The brothers, he deduced by the clamor of instruments, had somehow gotten loose from the ropes the audience had used to bind them. *They* were on the loose in there—making a racket with musical instruments—not spirits.

The Davenports were persuasive performers, and no one believed Maskelyne when he spoke up after the show. So with help from friend and cabinetmaker

George Alfred Cooke, he built a spirit cabinet of his own to re-create the spectacle. The friends teamed up to publicly expose the Davenport brothers later the same year, and five days afterward, the *Birmingham Gazette* cheered their act, pronouncing the Davenport brothers finished.

Maskelyne took the raves and went on to become one of England's best-loved magicians, regularly debunking false mediums and re-creating their phenomena in his act.

Not all magicians were antagonistic to Spiritualism, including Houdini's chief rival, the magician who had inherited Harry Kellar's secrets when the elder magician retired: Howard Thurston.

Thurston did his share of debunking but also championed some mediums as genuine. The Society of American Magicians (SAM) advised a hands-off approach when it came to phony psychics. The renewed interest in Spiritualism after World War I and the success of phenomena like spirit photographs had spilled over into the magic trade. Many magicians, including Thurston, used ghostly photography in their advertising, and because the two fields overlapped in so many ways, exposing the secrets of mediums often meant exposing the secrets of magicians, a grave professional offense. Magicians didn't rat out other magicians.

SAM's general rule: if an effect could be achieved in broad daylight, it fell under the category of magic; if it called for darkness, it was in the mediums' domain and open for debunking. (Houdini broke this rule while serving as SAM's president, revealing the workings of a "talking teakettle" in a 1922 article for *Popular Radio* magazine. The kettle, which spoke in a ghostly whisper and revealed secrets from the stage, was more a magician's trick than a tool of mediums, and he had bought the kettle in a magic shop. It took him a while to live this error down.)

Like Houdini, Thurston had no tolerance for outright exploitation. In an article titled "Thurston Will Wage Fight on Psychic

Detail from a spirit portrait on display at the Lily Dale Spiritualist Assembly museum in Western New York, thought to be created by the Bangs Sisters.

 Artful Spirits

Howard Thurston had great success with a Spirit Paintings act borrowed from the Bangs sisters, two Chicago spirit mediums. He would display a stack of blank canvases to the audience before holding one in front of a bright electric light, inviting a volunteer to suggest a subject or departed spirit, whose portrait gradually emerged on the canvas, first in misty lines, then in full detail and bold color. When Thurston removed the canvas from the backlighting, it was fully painted and dried. Audiences gaped in wonder.

Many Spiritualists believed the dead could write, draw, or paint through psychic channels. One Victorian medium, Georgiana Houghton, would host séances, enter a trance, and, with help from her spirit guide, make rich, surreal watercolors. Neglected by the art world as an eccentric in her lifetime, Houghton—or her work—enjoyed a revival a century and a half later when her spirit drawings were exhibited in London in 2016 and compared to works of the famous painter Kandinsky.

Fakes," he shared choice tidbits like this: "The most common form of ghosts used by the fraudulent spiritualists is contained in a small watch. It is blown up by a collapsible rod, which appears to be an ordinary lead pencil. This ghost can be made to do any of the stunts used by the mediums. It can be deflated quickly by use of the same rod." And he agreed with Houdini about Sir Arthur: "I find that Doyle has been badly duped. He is one of the easiest men I have met to mystify."

> "Fortune telling and *mind reading are all rot. Why read a palm for a dollar when you can forecast the stock market tomorrow.*" —HOWARD THURSTON

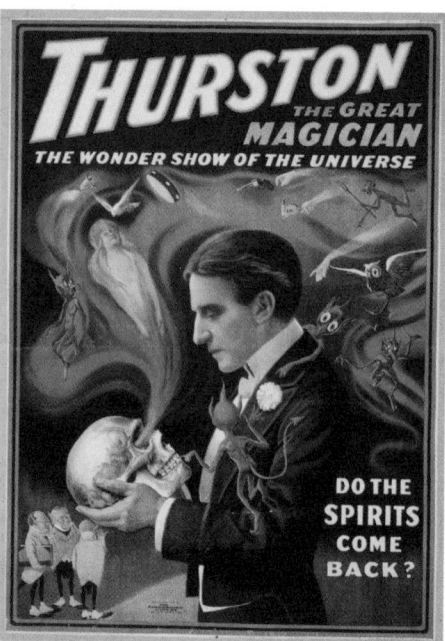

Theatrical poster advertising the magician Howard Thurston, 1915.

But in 1924 Houdini, the king of debunkers, found a formidable rival in Mina Stinson Crandon, known by her medium name, Margery.

Margery and her husband, Le Roi Goddard Crandon, a respected surgeon and Harvard faculty member, held séances at their home at 10 Lime Street in Boston. At first these were of the usual order—rapping and table tipping, music issuing from invisible instruments, sometimes with cameras documenting the proceedings—but in June 1923, Margery dropped into a trance, and a guide or "control" emerged. The gruff discarnate male voice belonged, Margery said, to her brother Walter, who had been killed in a train accident more than a decade before.

Walter ran the show from then on, issuing orders and overseeing trance writing and allowing his hand to be "captured" in a paraffin wax mold.

At the end of 1924, Margery produced her first ectoplasm, and it was no dainty cheesecloth wearing a face clipped from a magazine. It was bizarre and blubbery, definitely organic. Margery went on

Mina Crandon, known as the medium Margery, in 1924.

to "materialize" a hand, and Walter even managed to stamp his thumbprint in a tray of warm dental wax.

A year later, somebody located one of Walter's prints on a razor in a box in his mother's attic. Was it a match? It seemed to be, and like Mumler's first spirit photograph, it was proclaimed a miracle by many, indisputable evidence of immortality.

The story spread and attracted investigators, including William McDougall, head of the psychology department at Harvard, who got the inquiry rolling and had his doubts.

FIGURE 2.

"Walter's" thumbprint, 1932.

The magazine *Scientific American*, meanwhile, had announced a prize of $2,500 to anyone who could produce an "objective psychic manifestation of physical character" for an elite committee featuring Walter Franklin Prince, principal investigator for the ASPR, and Houdini.

"I am amused by your investigation with the Society for Psychical Research," said Sir Arthur Conan Doyle, when he learned that his onetime friend would participate, raising an old question between them. "Have they never thought of investigating you?"

Along with other people who had witnessed Houdini's death-defying performances over the years, Sir Arthur remained convinced that Houdini's talents were supernatural. Like the baffling Davenport Brothers, Houdini harbored a "dematerializing and reconstructing force," Sir Arthur had proposed, a force capable of separating "the molecules of that solid object toward which it is directed." How else to explain the "wonderful power" that turned handcuffs and straitjackets to putty—or thin air—in Houdini's hands?

Houdini in disguise, 1925.

"My methods are perfectly natural," Houdini insisted in *A Magician Among the Spirits*, "resting on natural laws of physics." These and all of his effects were just "superior" tricks.

Though Doyle generally did his best to be civil, in private he told *Scientific American* that Houdini would "keep away every decent medium—for they are human beings, not machines, and resent insult. . . . They do not go into an atmosphere which is antagonistic."

Margery agreed, in the end, to demonstrate her powers for the committee, although Houdini's reputation certainly preceded him: his quest to debunk frauds had become a full-on crusade. He would attend (and bust up) séances in elaborate disguises, disrupt mediums at work, and, to their shock and dismay, re-create their tricks. His lectures had turned countless people against "the cult," and in 1926, he would even testify to a packed and hostile audience—with Bess as a character witness—before Senate and House subcommittees for a bill prosecuting those "pretending to tell fortunes for reward or compensation."

MR. HOUDINI: Step this way, Mrs. Houdini. One of the witnesses said I was a brute and that I was vile and I was crazy. Won't you step this way? I want the chairman to see you. . . . There are no medals and no ribbons on me, but when a girl will stick to a man for 32 years as she did and when she will starve with me and work with me through thick and thin, it is a pretty good recommendation. Outside of my great mother, Mrs. Houdini has been my greatest friend. Have I shown traces of being crazy, unless it was about you? [Laughter]

MRS. HOUDINI: No.

MR. HOUDINI: Am I brutal to you, or vile?

MRS. HOUDINI: No. . . .

MR. HOUDINI: Thank you, Mrs. Houdini.
[Applause.]

—From court transcript of the Houdinis'
testimony at Senate and House subcommittee
hearings held over four days in February and
May 1926

Houdini's exposé of the medium
Margery, 1924.

Houdini had a special spirit cabinet built—the "Margie Box," as it came to be nicknamed—to contain the Boston medium's physical movements and limit her freedom to manipulate the séance environment. The committee observed twenty séances, and the debate lasted for a year.

The editor in charge of the story at *Scientific American*, J. Malcolm Bird, was so quickly convinced Margery was legitimate that he published a glowing report even before the committee convened. Houdini—who *wasn't* convinced and challenged her aggressively every step of the way—cried foul, and a firestorm began in the press, dividing the psychical research community and inspiring Houdini to publish, at his own expense, a pamphlet exposing her methods.

Early in 1925, he challenged Margery to appear with him at Boston's Symphony Hall, but the medium refused. Houdini held a séance in her absence, exposing her methods, and in the end, *Scientific American* declined to award Margery the prize on insufficient evidence. Some believed the medium was the most important of all time, others that she was a brazen fraud.

Margery also nearly duped an investigator from the London SPR office (who followed up with twenty-nine sittings), at first, but he eventually proved that her ectoplasm was shaped animal lung tissue. And Walter's thumbprint? Later investigations revealed that it belonged to Margery's dentist.

Mina Crandon would die, discredited, in 1941, but her performance—the long, strange puzzle of her success—echoed through the research community for years to come, her stubborn standoff with Houdini becoming the stuff of legend.

Investigative committee members Houdini, J. Malcolm Bird, and O. D. Munn with the medium Margery, July 24, 1924.

TEN

The End (or Is It?)

"I have never received a word."

∼Harry Houdini

At the end of 1925, *HOUDINI* opened on Broadway.

At two and a half hours, with three acts, it was the longest show he had performed, and it spanned his range, from iconic escapes to fifteen new tricks and illusions. The show would run several months and even opened for a time in Chicago, a suitably grand finale for a performer who became legend in his own lifetime.

Rounding out escapes and magic, Act 3, "Do the Dead Come Back?" was a spirit exposé—the combined proofs and musings of a man who had tirelessly devoted his life to wondering: was it possible? To not only survive but return from death?

"Mine has not been an investigation of a few days or weeks or months," he wrote in *A Magician Among the Spirits*, "but one that has extended over thirty years." The work of those three decades had convinced him, without doubt: "Everything that I have investigated has been the result of deluded brains or those which were too actively and intensely willing to believe."

Willing something to be true doesn't make it so, of course, and it may be that Houdini's fierce efforts to show up fraud were less about skepticism than hope. There's no doubt he *wanted* to believe. He wanted it very much. Perhaps the integrity of that hope was sacred, worth defending.

IN LATE OCTOBER OF 1926, HOUDINI ALLOWED A McGill University student in Montreal to punch him in the gut, as hard as possible. It was a test of strength, a test the muscled magician was well able, as a rule, to pass. But the punch came quickly, too quickly, and Houdini buckled under it. Despite the pain, he refused to see a doctor or cancel performances.

Houdini with boxers Jack Dempsey and Benny Leonard, 1920.

A week later, he collapsed after a show in Detroit. He was rushed to the hospital and diagnosed with a ruptured appendix, peritonitis, and a strep infection.

A few days and two operations later, Houdini died on Halloween, and was buried beside his mother in Cypress Hills Cemetery in Queens.

Over the years, he had quietly conspired with important people in his life: whoever died first would communicate with the other *if it were possible*. "I had compacts with a round dozen. Each one promised me faithfully to come back. . . . I have even gone so far as to create secret codes and handgrips."

The day before Houdini's private secretary, John W. Sargent (with whom he was very close), died, Sargent told him, "Houdini, this may be the end. If it is, I am coming back to you no matter what happens on the other side." They agreed that if he could, Sargent would relay all the secrets of the Beyond. But one word would be enough, a word they agreed upon in advance. Their minds and intentions were so aligned, Houdini believed, that his friend's message could not fail to find him if it were possible to send one. Another friend, the ninety-year-old niece of President Pierce, Atlanta Hall, clasped Houdini's hand on her deathbed, giving him their "agreed-upon grip which she was to give me through a medium."

Hall, like Sargent and others, held her silence in death.

"They have never come back to me!" Houdini said. "They were all loves, each strong, each binding. If these persons, with all the love they bore in their heart for me and all the love I have . . . did not return . . . Why," he pleaded, "should [other people's loved ones] come back and mine not?" How "wonderful" it would be to converse again with his dear mother.

"Sir Arthur Conan Doyle has repeatedly told the Spiritualists that I will eventually see the light and embrace Spiritualism. . . .

But if Spiritualism is to be founded on the tricks of exposed mediums, feats of magic, resort to trickery, then I say unflinchingly that I do not believe, and more, I will not believe. I have said many times that I am willing."

Honoring Houdini's dying wish, Bess Houdini held a séance every Halloween for ten years, on the anniversary of his death, to conjure his spirit, or try to. She sponsored her last séance in 1936. Others have picked up the mantle, and though no one has succeeded in establishing contact, the custom continues, to this day, at various séance tables around the world.

If it were possible—or even if it weren't—Houdini would be the first to tell us.

Bess Houdini, seated, hosts her final Houdini séance in 1936 in hope of contacting her dead husband.

FINIS

❖ *NOTES* ❖

Introduction

"'Impossibility commences'": *Spellbinder: The Life of Harry Houdini* by Tom Lalicki, p. 19.

"'mystifier of mystifiers'": *A Magician Among the Spirits* (*MAtS*) by Harry Houdini, p. xiv.

"eclipsing sensation": *Houdini!!! The Career of Ehrich Weiss* by Kenneth Silverman, title page.

"every country on the globe": http://memory.loc.gov/diglib/ihas/loc.rbc .varshoud.3g03288/default.html.

"'duplication, explanation, imitation or contradiction.'": Lalicki, p. 19.

"'Houdini. That's Enough'": Lalicki, p. 6.

"Honorary Secretary of the Society for the Study of Supernormal Pictures.": *MAtS*, p. 126.

"Sainted Mother": *MAtS*, preface.

"I have not found one incident that savoured of the genuine.": *MAtS*, p. xix.

PART ONE: There Is No Death, There Are No Dead

"There Is No Death, There Are No Dead": Ella Wheeler Wilcox, "There Is No Death, There Are No Dead," *Complete Poetical Works of Ella Wheeler Wilcox*.

1: Harry and Bess Houdini, Spirit Mediums

"To me it was a lark.": *MAtS*, p. xi.

"'Great Wizard' . . . 'little vocalist'": Silverman, p. 18.

"'accompanied by the sexton . . . everyone sleeping in God's acre.'": Silverman, p. 300.

"greatest and finest Trunk Mystery the world has ever seen.": Library of

Congress, Prints and Photographs online catalog: http://www.loc.gov/pictures/item/2014636906/.

"'The Great Mystifier' . . . 'The Celebrated Psycrometic Clairvoyant.'": Silverman, p. 19.

"I appreciated the fact that I surprised my clients . . . understand the seriousness.": *MAtS*, p. xi.

"'like a king'": Silverman, p. 19.

"'You can open Omaha March . . . season.' . . . 'This wire changed my whole Life's journey.'": Silverman, p. 22.

THE HOUDINIS

"'cheap' . . . 'glorious'": Silverman, p. 10.

"'Darling One and Only' . . . 'on my pillow.'": Silverman, p. 73.

THE EFFECT

"'Now then . . . the—EFFECT.'": Silverman, p. 12.

"'Just think over this . . . THREE SECONDS!'": Silverman, p. 13.

MIRACULOUS MENTORS

"'You Can See His Heart Beat! You Can See His Blood Circulate!'": Silverman, p. 11.

"defiers of poisonous reptiles. . . . The dime museum is but a memory now.": *Miracle Mongers and Their Methods* by Harry Houdini, contents, p. 240.

2: *Dealings with the Dead*

"'Spiritualism is the Science . . . spirit world.'": Silverman, p. 247.

"'Mr. Splitfoot'": *Talking to the Dead: Kate and Maggie Fox and the Rise of Spiritualism* by Barbara Weisberg, p. 95.

"'Now do this just as I do'": Weisberg, p. 18.

"'the Medium Business—Spiritualism'": Silverman, p. 39.

"'With due modesty . . . my peer'": Silverman, p. 129.

"'I most certainly did not relish the idea . . . my admirers.'": Silverman, p. 254.

WHERE DO WE GO FROM HERE?

"like confessing a murder": http://www.lettersofnote.com/2009/09/it-is
-like-confessing-murder.html.

AN EARNEST, LIFELONG ENDEAVOR

"'guide and hero . . . earnest, life-long endeavor.'": Lalicki, p. 6.

"'The Shakespeare of Magic'": Silverman, p. 130.

"'prince of pilferers' . . . 'Magic Ever Published'": Silverman, p. 131.

"'a mere pretender . . . brainwork of others.'": Silverman, p. 130.

"'a complete regeneration . . . supreme egotism.'": Silverman, p. 131.

FIFTY-FIVE KINGS

"'If you throw a stone in the air . . . in his pocket.'": Silverman, p. 63.

"'If you are in a fight . . . other guy first.'": Silverman, p. 69.

3: The Mother's Boy

"'I who have laughed . . . I do not think recovery is possible.'": Silverman,
p. 181.

"'the Great Dissolution was gradually taking place' . . . 'All right,
Mama.'": Silverman, p. 179.

"still and quiet . . . 'bowed down'": Silverman, p. 181.

"Sainted Mother": *MAtS*, preface.

"'a prayer' . . . 'Prisoner!'": Silverman, p. 183.

"'My very Existence' . . . 'ambition'": Silverman, p. 184.

"'I am what would be called a Mothers-boy' . . . 'Ma would want me to
do this?'": Silverman, p. 182.

"'It was a shame the way I had to fool him'": Silverman, p. 189.

"'man to man' . . . 'hokus pokus.'": Silverman, p. 190.

"'The Home is a Home . . . disposed of.'": Silverman, pp. 190–91.

"'Here I am left alone on the station . . . *join my mother.*'": Silverman, p. 190.

"'The easiest way to attract . . . sudden death.'": Silverman, p. 197.

"'work entirely'": Silverman, p. 202.

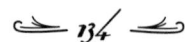

"MA SAW ME JUMP!"

"'The less said on the subject the better'": Lalicki, p. 4.

"'insignificant'": Silverman, p. 181.

"'Ma saw me jump!'": Silverman, p. 182.

I WANT TO BE FIRST

"'puny attempts at duplication'": Silverman, p. 66.

"'I want to be first . . . my life only for that.'": Lalicki, p. 55.

4: The Torch Bearer

"'I do not say that I think . . . I should not be sane.'": *The Adventures of Arthur Conan Doyle: A Biography* by Russell Miller, p. 413.

"'recognition, perhaps friendship, at the firesides throughout the world . . . torch bearer of spiritualism.'": Silverman, p. 250.

"'new Revelation' . . . 'the most important development in the history of the human race'": Silverman, p. 250.

"'Spiritualism is a humbug . . . brought into such a life.'": *The Death-Blow to Spiritualism: Being the True Story of the Fox Sisters, as Revealed by Authority of Margaret Fox Kane and Catherine Fox Jencken* by Reuben Briggs Davenport, p. 57.

"'I am afraid that I cannot say . . . by the spirits.'": Silverman, p. 253.

"'mystifier of mystifiers'": MAtS, p. xiv.

"I view these so-called phenomena . . . investigator.": MAtS, p. xiv.

"'I am seeking truth . . . this matter seriously.'": Silverman, p. 253.

"'no possible chance for trickery.'": Silverman, p. 255.

"My mind has always been open and receptive": MAtS, p. xiii.

"'Something must come your way if you really persevere . . . follows a rat.'": Silverman, p. 255.

"'the Etheric Body'": Silverman, p. 273.

"beyond any doubt": MAtS, p. 143.

"'In spite of the imagination of his writings . . . a crowd which had its dead.'": http://www.prairieghosts.com/doyle_houdini.html.

"'pathetic' . . . 'senile.'": Miller, pp. 413–14.

"a deep thinker . . . this great author.": *MAtS*, p. 138.

"'The children would teach you to swim'": Silverman, p. 280.

"'might come through.'": Miller, p. 424.

"'our friends from beyond.'": Miller, p. 424.

"religious . . . I made up my mind . . . presence of my beloved Mother.": *MatS*, pp. 151–52.

"'Oh my darling . . . rest in peace.'": Silverman, p. 282.

"'tossing each to Houdini . . . every moment.'": Miller, p. 424.

"'deeply moved' . . . 'have the nerve.'": Silverman, p. 283.

"surrendered themselves . . . the most monstrous fiction.": *MAtS*, preface.

DECEPTION ∼ OR CONSOLATION?

"'horrible deception' . . . 'the death blow'": *MAtS*, p. 5.

THE POWER BEHIND THE THRONE

"'the power behind the throne'": *Houdini: Art and Magic* by Brooke Kamin Rapaport, p. 92.

5: *"In the Light"*

"'Some persons . . . "and we will believe otherwise"?'": *MAtS*, p. 35.

"'The darkness of the theater . . . weird effect upon the crowd.'": *The Witch of Lime Street: Séance, Seduction, and Houdini in the Spirit World* by David Jaher, p. 60.

"'being of a jovial disposition, always ready for a joke'": *The Strange Case of William Mumler, Spirit Photographer* by Louis Kaplan, pp. 71–72.

"'This photograph was taken . . . twelve years since.'": Kaplan, pp. 35–36.

"'humble instrument . . . surrounds us.'": Kaplan, p. 69.

"'low swindle.'": Kaplan, p. 1.

"'palming off, as genuine spirit likenesses . . . living in this city'": Kaplan, p. 58.

"'Man is naturally both credulous . . . taken advantage.'": Kaplan, p. 155.

"'a man with an angel . . . just as I wish.'": Kaplan, p. 191.

"'Have you never' . . . 'with it sometimes.'": Kaplan, p. 197.

"'Persons of all classes . . . "A miracle."'": Kaplan, p. 188.

"'Let me say to you . . . spiritually yours.'": Kaplan, p. 184.

"'morally'": Kaplan, p. 206.

"much annoyed at his premature . . . Spirit world." *MAtS*, p. 122.

"'a very good likeness . . . to see my son again.'": Silverman, p. 273.

"would keep him busy for months": *MAtS*, p. 129.

"'the greatest spirit photo ever taken.'": Silverman, p. 273.

"From a logical, rational point of view . . . take the reward.": *MAtS*, pp. 136–37.

"'Poor, dear, loveable . . . heart of a child.'": Miller, p. 409.

HOW TO SHOOT SPIRITS

"regular . . . additional hazy something": *MAtS*, p. 115.

AIRY IMAGES

"'air images'": *Magic, 1400s–1950s*, edited by Noel Daniel, p. 162.

FAIRIES ON FILM

"proving the existence of fairies . . . opening the way to a new world": *The Perfect Medium: Photography and the Occult* by Clément Chéroux and Andreas Fischer, p. 93.

"'Among all the notable persons attracted to Spiritualism . . . honesty.'": Miller, p. 409.

6: *Manifestations!*

"'Strange how people imagine things in the dark . . . over their heads.'": *MAtS*, p. 25.

"'The best' . . . 'ridiculous stuff.'": Silverman, p. 255.

"'She was afraid of me' . . . 'quite final?'": Silverman, p. 255.

"'You have a reputation among Spiritualists of being a bitterly prejudiced enemy . . . humble spirit.'": *MAtS*, p. 164.

"'forces beyond . . . impulse of sympathy'": *MAtS*, p. 162.

"'You are a magnificent actor . . . beneath a man of your talent.'": Silverman, p. 256.

"scoffing . . . against any trickery.": *MatS*, p. 168.

"lady members of the Committee . . . adhering to her veil on the inside.": *MAtS*, p. 169.

"almost identical . . . manipulate my experiment.": *MAtS*, p. 170.

"a subtle and gifted assistant . . . honest": *MAtS*, p. 172.

"wrong in the air": *MAtS*, p. 171.

"in a blank . . . an atmosphere of incredulity": *MAtS*, p. 267.

"'If you want to send a telegram . . . office'": *MAtS*, p. 268.

"simply took advantage . . . nature": *MAtS*, p. 172.

"authentically classified as questionable": *MAtS*, p. 179.

"nothing beyond the simple act of regurgitation . . . 'medium's pocket.'": *MAtS*, p. 172.

"He treats Spiritualism as a religion . . . the deed.": *MAtS*, pp. 140–41.

"the future state of a soul.": *MAtS*, p. 177.

"horrible, revolting . . . stunts.": *MAtS*, p. 179.

"began a new line of psychical research": *MAtS*, p. xii.

"reality to the return . . . brain power I possess": *MAtS*, pp. xi–xii.

"trifling with the hallowed reverence . . . departed": *MAtS*, p. xi.

"I too would have parted gladly . . . bestowed.": *MAtS*, p. xi.

"realized that it bordered on crime.": *MAtS*, p. xi.

"a séance room except with an open mind.": *MAtS*, p. xii.

"involuntary and subconscious": *MAtS*, p. 110.

"I have attended . . . monotony.": *MAtS*, p. 110.

"just at the psychological moment . . . were two acrobats.": *MAtS*, p. 113.

"preferably cobweb-fine French muslin": *Ghost Hunters: William James and the Search for Scientific Proof of Life After Death* by Deborah Blum, p. 29.

"greatly in debt . . . certain documents": *MAtS*, p. 223.

"If it is possible to steal the records . . . of a family.": *MAtS*, p. 220.

"the 'gilded lobster palaces' of Broadway": *MAtS*, p. 218.

"a quiet couple . . . handsomely the first year.": *MAtS*, p. 221.

"Under the excitement . . . escape the medium.": *MAtS*, p. 223.

"human wolves": *MAtS*, p. 221.

"human leeches": *MAtS*, p. 190.

"human vultures": *MAtS*, p. 217.

"resourceful in obtaining information . . . their victims.": *MAtS*, p. 217.

WATER-TORTURE CELL ESCAPE

"'the greatest sensational mystery ever attempted in this or any age'":
   Lalicki, p. 43.

EATING NEEDLES ON A STRING

"'taking iron for the blood' . . . 'snap under his iron teeth.'": Silverman,
   p. 24.

SPIRIT WORDSMITHS

"'Any mechanical deception or sleight-of-hand . . . impossible.'":
   Silverman, p. 251.

7: *A Menace to Health and Sanity*

"'How long a private friendship can survive . . . the situation.'": *Final
   Séance: The Strange Friendship Between Houdini and Conan Doyle* by
   Massimo Polidoro, p. 186.

"possibility of communication . . . gone beyond.'": Silverman, p. 291.

"'I saw what you got . . . at the time.'": Jaher, p. 95.

"'I have no fancy . . . in public.'": Jaher, p. 94.

"'I have done my best to give you the truth . . . friendly converse.'": *MatS*,
   p. 157.

"'You write that you are very sore . . . other human beings.'": Jaher, p. 95.

"'I read an interview . . . wonder how you reconcile your various utter-
   ances!'": Polidoro, p. 168.

"'Our relations are certainly curious . . . attack you in turn.'": *MatS*, p. 164.

"'Sir Arthur Coming to Answer Houdini'": Silverman, p. 293.

"'harmless and ingenious . . . airs of superior intelligence.'": Silverman,
   p. 294.

"'Houdini, the magician . . . Wait till Sir A. C. Doyle hears of my lectures!'": Silverman, 298.

"no warfare": *MAtS*, p. 165.

"craze": *MAtS*, p. xvi.

"cult": *MAtS*, p. 207.

"a menace to health and sanity.": *MAtS*, p. xvi.

"who declared herself in love . . . join him.": *MAtS*, p. 181.

"'Wife Seeks Death . . . Husband from Beyond.'": Stashower, p. 373.

"'The incident shows the great danger . . . spiritual matters.'": Polidoro, p. 178.

"'communication . . . five children to her.'": *MAtS*, p. 182.

"It is with the deepest interest and concern . . . bereavement.": *MAtS*, p. xvi.

"'Truth wins and there is lots of time.'": *MAtS*, p. 163.

"'The first thing the knowledge . . . happy than the earth-life.'": *Our Second American Adventure* by Arthur Conan Doyle, p. 31.

"'broken down . . . a solace to their feelings'": *MAtS*, p. xvii.

"asylums would be flooded . . . diversions.": *MAtS*, p. 190.

"'People have been going mad . . . besides Spiritualism.'": *MAtS*, p. 143.

"realize the suffering, losses . . . curse.": *MAtS*, p. 180.

"The *Washington Times* . . . 'Alfred's Spiritual guidance.'": *MAtS*, pp. 181–82.

"the majority of people who are fleeced . . . among thieves.": *MAtS*, p. 227.

"adventurers . . . obtained by these two": *MAtS*, p. 67.

"one of the most extraordinary fake mediums . . . the world.": *MAtS*, p. 66.

"the daughter of King Louis I . . . thousands of dollars.": *MAtS*, p. 67.

"whose work, in spite . . . proof of Spiritualism.": *MAtS*, p. 38.

"'We were touched by the invisible.'": Blum, p. 22.

"a life of positive luxury . . . earthly sustenance": *MAtS*, p. 39.

"custom of living . . . dupes.": *MAtS*, p. 40.

"dematerialize . . . rematerialize": *MAtS*, p. 44.

"saturated with delusion . . . superstitious.": *MAtS*, p. 46.

"The average medium . . . stopped.": *MAtS*, p. 190.

FINGERPRINTING A SPIRIT

"startling swindles . . . sort of fraud.": *MAtS*, p. 115.

HOW DO I DISTRUST THEE? LET ME COUNT THE WAYS

"'Now, don't, sir! . . . was truth'": *The Table-Rappers: The Victorians and the Occult* by Ronald Pearsall, p. 97.

OUT ONE WINDOW, IN THE OTHER

"under the same conditions . . . laws of physics.": *MAtS*, pp. 48–49.

8: Science and Sincerity

"Psychical science, as we here try to pursue it . . . world of thought.": *Presidential Addresses to the Society for Psychical Research, 1882–1911*, p. 86.

"Gladly would I embrace . . . claims": *MAtS*, preface.

"serious-minded . . . pseudo-mediums.": *Miracle Mongers*, pp. 96–97.

"fortified . . . grief.": *MAtS*, p. xviii.

"perfect willingness . . . deceived": *MAtS*, p. 216.

"'The objective side . . . the matter.'": *MAtS*, pp. 207–8.

"permit his pen . . . moved to compassion": *MAtS*, p. 206.

"'DOYLE IN DENVER' . . . 'blasphemous and absurd.'": Silverman, p. 295.

"'There is nothing that Sir Arthur will believe' . . . 'not friendly.'": Silverman, p. 297.

"There is not the slightest doubt . . . hoodwinked": *MAtS*, p. 205.

"immune . . . *magnetism*": *MAtS*, p. 47.

"fairer-minded . . . impartial": *MAtS*, p. 193.

"deeply impressed . . . levity.": Seybert Commission, "Preliminary Report of the Commission Appointed by the University of Pennsylvania to Investigate Modern Spiritualism in Accordance with the Request of the Late Henry Seybert," p. 3.

"No one . . . barred": Seybert, p. 85.

"an unwillingness . . . difficult and expensive.": Seybert, p. 135.

"this phenomenon . . . legerdemain": Seybert, p. 105.

"We . . . single novel fact.": Seybert, p. 125.

"'science ignored . . . could not explain.'": Blum, p. 40.

"'you will find . . . surface of history.'": Blum, p. 25.

"'Something hit me . . . you still!'": Blum, p. 97.

"'universal proposition . . . ears and wits'": Blum, p. 204.

"I am not a scoffer . . . first to acknowledge my mistake.": *MAtS*, p. 179.

9: It Takes a Flimflammer to Catch a Flimflammer

"All mediums hate . . . séance.": *MAtS*, p. 192.

"contributions . . . even to punctuation.": *MAtS*, pp. 83–84.

"one of our number . . . writing the answer.": Seybert, p. 16.

"the only way to conduct a successful [investigation] . . . rehearsed.": *MAtS*, p. 192.

"'an eminent professional juggler' . . . 'manifestations are'": *MAtS*, pp. 86–87.

"'It is much more lucrative . . . honest magician.'": Daniel, p. 191.

"the grave scientist . . . logic.": *MAtS*, p. 60.

"with my own eyes . . . ears": *MAtS*, p. 208.

"on good authority . . . conduct.": *MAtS*, pp. 50–51.

"mal-observation . . . subconscious mind.": *MAtS*, pp. 191–92.

"This love of the dead . . . experiments": Young, James C. "Magic and Mediums: Houdini, Man of Many Tricks, Tells of Duplicating Feats of Spirit Workers—All 'Revelations' Easy to Explain," *New York Times*, May 7, 1922.

"One little sign even . . . converted.": *MAtS*, p. xvi.

"unusual for the eye . . . tricks.": *MAtS*, p. xv.

"deceived once . . . observer be.": *MAtS*, p. xviii.

"'Fortune telling and mind reading . . . stock market tomorrow.'": *The Last Greatest Magician in the World: Howard Thurston Versus Houdini and the Battles of the American Wizards* by Jim Steinmeyer, p. 287.

"'The most common . . . met to mystify.'": Steinmeyer, *The Last Greatest Magician*, p. 287.

"objective psychic manifestation of physical character": Silverman, p. 313.

"'I am amused . . . investigating you?'": *MAtS*, p. 163.

"dematerializing and reconstructing . . . wonderful power": Silverman, p. 259.

"My methods . . . superior.": *MAtS*, pp. 211–14.

"'keep away every decent medium . . . antagonistic.'": Jaher, p. 96.

"'pretending to tell fortunes . . . compensation.'": Silverman, p. 392.

"'MR. HOUDINI . . . Applause.'": Silverman, p. 396.

ON TO SAFER SWINDLES

"Spirit slates . . . 'ouija board.'": *MAtS*, p. 79.

WHY DID THEY DO IT?

"in her crafty prime . . . producer.": *MAtS*, pp. 64–65.

SUPPLYING PECULIAR EFFECTS

"'Our experience . . . the entire world.'": http://www.prairieghosts.com/gambols.html.

10: The End (or Is It?)

"I have never received a word.": *MAtS*, p. xii.

"Mine has not been . . . willing to believe.": *MAtS*, p. xix.

"I had compacts with a round dozen . . . handgrips.": *MAtS*, p. 269.

"'Houdini, this may be the end . . . side.'": *MAtS*, p. xiii.

"agreed-upon grip . . . back to me!": *MAtS*, p. 269.

"They were all loves . . . that I am willing.": *MAtS*, p. 270.

❖ BIBLIOGRAPHY ❖

Blum, Deborah. *Ghost Hunters: William James and the Search for Scientific Proof of Life After Death*. New York: Penguin, 2006.

Chéroux, Clément, and Andreas Fischer. *The Perfect Medium: Photography and the Occult*. New Haven and London: Yale University Press, 2005.

Daniel, Noel, ed. *Magic, 1400s–1950s*. 2009. Reprint, Cologne: Taschen, 2015.

Davenport, Reuben Briggs. *The Death-Blow to Spiritualism: Being the True Story of the Fox Sisters, as Revealed by Authority of Margaret Fox Kane and Catherine Fox Jencken*. New York: G. W. Dillingham, 1888.

Doyle, Arthur Conan. *Our Second American Adventure*. London: Hodder and Stoughton, 1924.

Houdini, Harry. *Houdini Exposes the Tricks Used by the Boston Medium "Margery" to Win the $2500 Prize Offered by the* Scientific American. New York: Adams Press, 1924.

_____. *A Magician Among the Spirits*. 1924. Reprint, Amsterdam: Fredonia Books, 2002.

_____. *Miracle Mongers and Their Methods: A Complete Exposé*. 1920. Reprint, New York: Prometheus Books, 1981.

_____. "Silent Second Sight." *Mahatma* 1, no. 12 (June 1898).

Jaher, David. *The Witch of Lime Street: Séance, Seduction, and Houdini in the Spirit World*. New York: Crown, 2015.

Kaplan, Louis. *The Strange Case of William Mumler, Spirit Photographer*. Minneapolis: University of Minnesota Press, 2008.

Lalicki, Tom. *Spellbinder: The Life of Harry Houdini*. New York: Holiday House, 2000.

Lamont, Peter. *The First Psychic: The Peculiar Mystery of a Notorious Victorian Wizard*. London: Little, Brown, 2005.

Miller, Russell. *The Adventures of Arthur Conan Doyle: A Biography*. New York: Thomas Dunne Books, 2008.

Pearsall, Ronald. *The Table-Rappers: The Victorians and the Occult*. Gloucestershire: Sutton Publishing, 2004.

Polidoro, Massimo. *Final Séance: The Strange Friendship Between Houdini and Conan Doyle*. New York: Prometheus Books, 2001.

Rapaport, Brooke Kamin. *Houdini: Art and Magic*. New York: The Jewish Museum; New Haven: Yale University Press, 2010.

Redniss, Lauren. *Radioactive: Marie and Pierre Curie; A Tale of Love and Fallout*. New York: HarperCollins, 2011.

Roach, Mary. *Spook: Science Tackles the Afterlife*. New York: Norton, 2005.

Silverman, Kenneth. *Houdini!!! The Career of Ehrich Weiss*. New York: HarperCollins, 1996.

Society for Psychical Research (Great Britain). *Presidential Addresses to the Society for Psychical Research, 1882–1911*. Glasgow: Glasgow University Press, 1912.

Stashower, Daniel. *Teller of Tales: The Life of Arthur Conan Doyle*. New York: Henry Holt, 1999.

Steinmeyer, Jim. *Hiding the Elephant: How Magicians Invented the Impossible and Learned to Disappear*. New York: Carroll & Graf, 2003.

_____. *The Last Greatest Magician in the World: Howard Thurston Versus Houdini and the Battles of the American Wizards*. New York: Penguin, 2011.

Weisberg, Barbara. *Talking to the Dead: Kate and Maggie Fox and the Rise of Spiritualism*. San Francisco: HarperSanFrancisco, 2004.

Widen, Larry, and Judi Anderson. *Silver Screens: A Pictorial History of Milwaukee's Movie Theaters*. Wisconsin: Milwaukee Historical Society Press, 2007.

WEBLIOGRAPHY

American Experience. "Houdini: The Man Behind the Myth." A companion website to the 2000 PBS Home Video. http://www.pbs.org/wgbh/amex/houdini/.

Cox, John. *Wild About Harry.* http://www.wildabouthoudini.com/.

Hodge, Brandon. *Mysterious Planchette.* http://mysteriousplanchette.blogspot.com.

Interval, Tom. "Houdini in the *New York Times*." http://www.houdinimuseum
.org/articles/1926_11.01.html.

Notaro, Joe. *Harry Houdini Circumstantial Evidence.*
http://harryhoudinicircumstantialevidence.com.

The Public Domain Review. http://publicdomainreview.org.

Seybert Commission. "Preliminary Report of the Commission Appointed by the
University of Pennsylvania to Investigate Modern Spiritualism in Accordance
with the Request of the Late Henry Seybert." eBook #11950: Project
Gutenberg, 2004. http://onlinebooks.library.upenn.edu/webbin/gutbook
/lookup?num=11950.

Taylor, Troy. "The Haunted Museum." http://www.prairieghosts.com/gambols
.html.

Young, James C. "Magic and Mediums: Houdini, Man of Many Tricks, Tells
of Duplicating Feats of Spirit Workers—All 'Revelations' Easy to Explain."
New York Times, May 7, 1922. Courtesy of Tom Interval,
http://www.houdinimuseum.org.

❈ ACKNOWLEDGMENTS ❈

Thanks to Lisa Goodfellow Bowe, first reader and all-around first person; my brilliant agent, Jill Grinberg; publisher Ken Wright, whose enthusiasm drove the project from the beginning; my wise and gracious editor, Alex Ulyett; designer Kate Renner, copyeditors Janet Pascal and Laura Stiers, proofreaders Ryan Sullivan and Krista Ahlberg, and the other talented folk at Viking. Magicians, all.

Thanks, too, to Ken Silverman for his rich, invaluable biography—the gold standard—and to Kevin Connolly, John Cox, Joe Harris, Tom Interval, Brandon Hodge, Ron Nagy, Leslie Price, and Ken Trombly.

Last but not least, thanks to Mark Osterman of Eastman Museum, who taught me to photograph ghosts, and to my patient models, who endured the old, slow, moody, stinking wet-plate collodion process—usually in a hot barn, draped in gauze—with creativity, good cheer, and a surprising (under the circumstances) sense of fun: Lisa Goodfellow Bowe, John Bresnahan, Karin Goodfellow, Audra Jones, Paige Jones, Cecilia LeBlanc, Kathy Noyes LeBlanc, and Michaela Wayshak.

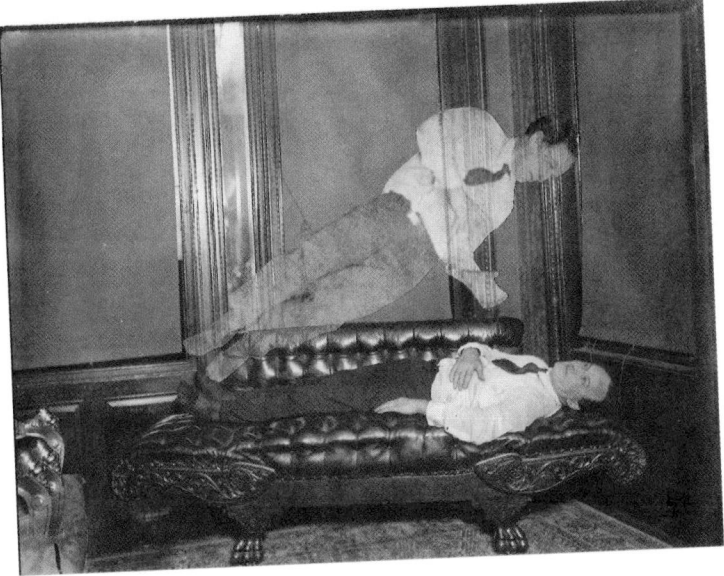

Spirit photograph/photo collage of Houdini, circa 1924.

❂ PICTURE CREDITS ❂

❖ INDEX ❖

Note: Page numbers in *italics* refer to illustrations.